The Parent's Guide to
Uncluttering
Your Home

How to Organize
What You Need and
Recycle What You Don't

Janet Morris Grimes

THE PARENT'S GUIDE TO UNCLUTTERING YOUR HOME: HOW TO ORGANIZE WHAT YOU NEED AND RECYCLE WHAT YOU DON'T

Copyright © 2011 Atlantic Publishing Group, Inc.
1405 SW 6th Avenue • Ocala, Florida 34471 • Phone 800-814-1132 • Fax 352-622-1875
Web site: www.atlantic-pub.com • E-mail: sales@atlantic-pub.com
SAN Number: 268-1250

Library of Congress Cataloging-in-Publication Data

Grimes, Janet Morris, 1967-
  The parent's guide to uncluttering your home : how to organize what you need and recycle what you don't / by Janet Morris Grimes.
     p. cm.
  ISBN-13: 978-1-60138-338-9 (alk. paper)
  ISBN-10: 1-60138-338-X (alk. paper)
  1. Storage in the home. 2. House cleaning. 3. Parents--Life skills guides. I. Title.
  TX309.G75 2010
  648'.5--dc22
                            2010037800

Printed in the United States

PROJECT MANAGER: Amy Moczynski • AMoczynski@atlantic-pub.com
PROOFREADER: Brett Daly • brett.daly1@gmail.com
INTERIOR LAYOUT: Antoinette D'Amore • addesign@videotron.ca
COVER DESIGNS: Jackie MIller • millerjackiej@gmail.com

Printed on Recycled Paper

We recently lost our beloved pet "Bear," who was not only our best and dearest friend but also the "Vice President of Sunshine" here at Atlantic Publishing. He did not receive a salary but worked tirelessly 24 hours a day to please his parents. Bear was a rescue dog that turned around and showered myself, my wife, Sherri, his grandparents Jean, Bob, and Nancy, and every person and animal he met (maybe not rabbits) with friendship and love. He made a lot of people smile every day.

We wanted you to know that a portion of the profits of this book will be donated to The Humane Society of the United States. *–Douglas & Sherri Brown*

The human-animal bond is as old as human history. We cherish our animal companions for their unconditional affection and acceptance. We feel a thrill when we glimpse wild creatures in their natural habitat or in our own backyard.

Unfortunately, the human-animal bond has at times been weakened. Humans have exploited some animal species to the point of extinction.

The Humane Society of the United States makes a difference in the lives of animals here at home and worldwide. The HSUS is dedicated to creating a world where our relationship with animals is guided by compassion. We seek a truly humane society in which animals are respected for their intrinsic value, and where the human-animal bond is strong.

Want to help animals? We have plenty of suggestions. Adopt a pet from a local shelter, join The Humane Society and be a part of our work to help companion animals and wildlife. You will be funding our educational, legislative, investigative and outreach projects in the U.S. and across the globe.

Or perhaps you'd like to make a memorial donation in honor of a pet, friend or relative? You can through our Kindred Spirits program. And if you'd like to contribute in a more structured way, our Planned Giving Office has suggestions about estate planning, annuities, and even gifts of stock that avoid capital gains taxes.

Maybe you have land that you would like to preserve as a lasting habitat for wildlife. Our Wildlife Land Trust can help you. Perhaps the land you want to share is a backyard— that's enough. Our Urban Wildlife Sanctuary Program will show you how to create a habitat for your wild neighbors.

So you see, it's easy to help animals. And The HSUS is here to help.

THE HUMANE SOCIETY
OF THE UNITED STATES.

2100 L Street NW • Washington, DC 20037 • 202-452-1100
www.hsus.org

Dedication

This book serves as proof that sometimes dreams chase you down until you are ready to surrender to their power. Appreciation for my husband, Thomas, for your patience, for your belief in me, and for putting up with the clutter the process of writing this book caused. To my kids, Crystal, Andrew, and Malloree, for giving me daily reasons to become an author. How could I not write about you? To my Mom and sister, Jeanna, for demonstrating perseverance and inner strength when no one but me was watching. I love you all.

Table of Contents

Foreword.. 11

Introduction 15

The Journey from Clutter to Clarity... 15

Where to Begin When it Seems Overwhelming 18

About this Book 19

Charting the Way Out 20

Oppress the Mess Tips 20

One Step at a Time 21

Chapter 1: Trapped in the Clutter Cycle 25

Assessing Your Mess..28

How Clutter Affects You and Your Family............................31

Understanding and Blending Personality Types 34

What Lies Behind the Pattern of Clutter 37

What You Tell Yourself Along the Way 38

Remove Your Obstacles..46

Rediscover Your Dignity 47

Chapter 2: When Your Stuff Owns You..............49

Obeying Your Stuff..51

Extreme Cases of Hoarding..51

How Much Stuff or Clutter Can You Afford? 52

Storage Industry Insanity 54

The Shopping Epidemic..57

Giving Yourself Permission to Change 61

Chapter 3: A Family Affair — Setting Yours Up for Success..............63

Parent versus Drill Sergeant...64

Getting the Family to Buy In...65

A Six-week Commitment..69

Chapter 4: Conquering Your Clutter Zones...................77

Uncluttering Your Home as if Placing it on the Market.......78

Room by Room Evaluation..82

Simple Entryway Solutions 86

Small Home Solutions 88

Uncluttering Family Areas..91

Chapter 5: Airing YourDirty Laundry 99

Establishing your Laundry System 99

Laundry Basics 103

De-Wrinkling Your Time — How to Prevent Wrinkles 112

Chapter 6: Claustrophobic Closets .. 115

Hidden Treasures 116

The Secret Weapon...118

Sticky Note Game..119

The Dreaded Bedroom Closets 120

Restoring Order 127

Storage for Seasonal Items..131

Coats, Linens, and Things..134

Chapter 7: Bedrooms and Broomsticks 139

Starting Seems to be the Hardest Part 143

The Magic of Children's Furniture 147

Uncluttering Your Kids' Stuff..149

The Chest, the Drawers, and the Wardrobe 152

Chapter 8: Bathroom Bingo — Rules of the Game 157

Take Inventory of Supplies 158

Storing Items on Your Terms 159

Weekly Bathroom Cleaning Tasks 161

Becoming Master of the Master Bath 164

Guest Bathrooms...167

Rules for the Kids' Bathroom 169

Chapter 9: Cutting the Kitchen Chaos 175

Open for Business, and When to Close...................................176

Refrigerator Magnets — Limiting the Pull of the Refrigerator on Your Family...176

Avoiding Freezer Burn 182

Cabinet Creations 184

Pantry Progress..189

Dishing it Out 195

Chapter 10: Attacking Your Attic, Basement, or Garage 199

Up or Down?..203

The Purpose of Your Garage...206

Eight Ways to Reclaim Your Car Space...................................209

Proper Disposal of Household Hazardous Waste 213

Chapter 11: New to the Recycling Movement.........................215

Making Treasures Out of Your Leftovers.............................216

Out-of-the-Box Donations...216

Chapter 12: Transforming Trash into Cash 223

Identifying the Different Types of Consignment or
Resale Options...225

Selling Everything but the Yard...227

Chapter 13: Uncluttering Your Office Space 233

Home Office Area..235

The Home Computer 239

Filing More Than Your Fingernails......................................241

Chapter 14: Keeping Your Home Running Smoothly...........................245

Set Up a Nightly Routine 245

12 Steps to Speed-cleaning While No one Else is Home ...247

How to Reduce Shopping Trips and Costs 252

Chapter 15: Honoring Your Past without Destroying Your Future 259

How to Handle Collectibles 260

Inheriting Family Treasures 266

Conclusion: Unclutter Your Mind 269

De-cluttering Your Life 270

Finding the Right Balance...271

Bibliography 273

Author Biography 283

Index 285

Foreword

Do you own your stuff, or does it own you? Do you have a two-car garage that houses everything but your car? If you answered a resounding yes and you are a parent, then Janet Morris Grimes' book *The Parent's Guide to Uncluttering Your Home* is for you!

Clutter is an issue that has no restrictions as to who suffers from its clutches, and if left unattended, clutter can cause stress, anxiety, and loss of time as you constantly look for something. Aside from that, you teach your children a bad habit they will take into adulthood. By getting a handle on your stuff and mandating a place for everything, you teach your children responsibility and skills they will take into adulthood — and your house will get organized now.

The battle over clutter is a battle all parents must deal with, especially if they do not have proper systems in place to begin with. The main struggle with parents is getting their kids in the habit of putting their stuff in its proper place. Kids learn from their parent's actions and behaviors; if parents do not put their stuff away, why should children? *The Parent's Guide to Uncluttering Your*

Home helps parents identify what processes are missing in their households and how to establish them with the six-week commitment, as well as how to help get the entire family on board and take back their home. The key is helping families break down what the problem is — including compulsive shopping, not putting stuff away the first time, and not having a designated place for the stuff— establishing a plan, and then breaking the home into clutter zones and deciding how to de-clutter and then reorganize them. Important tips are broken down into bullet points in the "Oppress the Mess" sidebars, which are extremely helpful, and in the checklists that help parents act as if they are getting their home ready for sale, which was one of my favorite parts of the book.

As owner of Bante Design LLC and the creator of The Clutter Counseling program, I highly recommend this book for any parent who wants to take back control of his or her stuff (and conversely, his or her life) and teach kids good organizational habits. This book serves as a guide for setting up an action plan to get all family members involved, a room-by-room checklist of what to tackle and how, and case studies to help illustrate each point with real-life examples that readers can identify with.

Happy Purging!

DeAnna Radaj
Bante Design LLC
Move Your Couch, Change Your Life

www.bantedesign.com
www.deannaradaj.com
info@bantedesign.com

DeAnna Radaj, owner of Bante Design LLC, is a nationally recognized speaker on healthy home design, color therapy/theory, psychology of clutter for adults and children, and a variety of business topics for the individual, small business owner, and entrepreneur. Her design philosophy entails designing spaces that are not only beautiful and comfortable but also spaces that bring out the client's personality. Visit the Bante Design website for a list of all workshops and appearances at **www.bantedesign.com***.*

The Journey from Clutter to Clarity

A cluttered lifestyle is as cumbersome as it sounds: un-
productive, unfocused, unimaginative, and unyielding.
When surrounded by clutter, this may be how you feel
about yourself, as well as your home. Any sparks of creativity
are quenched because there is no time or space to follow through
with your ideas. Constantly aware of what needs to be done, you
are never quite sure how or where to start. Any tasks you complete bring no sense of accomplishment because bigger, harder,
and messier tasks clamor for your attention. You go through the
motions and try to keep up, but at the end of the day, you wonder
if you accomplished anything at all.

If this is how you feel when living in a cluttered environment,
imagine what it does to your family. This is one of the most important reasons to gain control of your home. You need to recap-

ture your family's sense of fun and need to open their world to how motivated and focused they can be in the right environment. By understanding why your clutter has taken over your home and by chipping away at the problem one room at a time, you will be thrilled to discover the fulfilling lifestyle that waits for you. You will view your life through a renewed sense of clarity and focus and will be so thankful you took the steps to arrive at such a destination.

If the clutter in your home robs you from focusing on your children as they come in the door at the end of a hectic day, it is time to do something about it. If your home's current state presents a barrier between you and the friends and family you yearn to invite inside, then it is time to change. If the condition of your home is a sensitive topic between you and your spouse that frequently causes arguments, it is time to find a common middle ground to improve this condition. If you find yourself staying away from your home as long as possible so you will not be forced to confront your clutter, it is time to choose another course of action.

The cluttered lifestyle leads to confusion and a lack of focus for everyone involved. Clutter serves as a constant reminder of the lengthy list of what you still must do. When you surround yourselves with meaningless stuff, it becomes excess baggage, causing you to waste time and effort carrying it around with you. In order to recognize and identify patterns of clutter, you need to step back and seek a fresh point of view. As you seek a permanent lifestyle change, you must first take a complete inventory of the history of your habits, emotions, and physical possessions. It could be that your cluttered home reflects a cluttered heart and mind as well.

As your family grows, both in number as well as in physical size, so does the list of things you own. Any new parent marvels at the amount of equipment required to care for the baby: Bottles, food, toys, clothing, blankets, diapers, baby wipes, playpens or portable cribs, and high chairs take over your home when you welcome a new baby to the world. Then, as your children quickly outgrow their clothes, shoes, and toys, a parent can barely keep up with what is still usable and what is no longer needed. Without an outlined plan of action, any home will fall victim to the piles of stuff that accumulate as children grow. Having a family translates to a frenzied schedule that multiplies with each new addition. As you manage your family, keeping up with and supporting the activities of each child, little time remains to manage and maintain the home.

For those of you who find yourselves surrounded by clutter, the process of learning to control it may feel overwhelming. Not knowing where to start paralyzes you, preventing you from making any changes at all. This book is set up in such a way that it offers tips and ideas you can use at any time, and each step to improvement builds on another. However, it also establishes an introduction period where you family forms new habits. Beginning a difficult task is the hardest part, but by creating a launching point and then adding to it each day, you will progress further than you ever dreamed. Over time, you will learn what works for your family and how quickly you can make improvements to create a welcoming and uncluttered environment.

Where to Begin When it Seems Overwhelming

This book is an important first step in your journey from clutter to clarity. The journey requires you to take a few steps in the right direction each day. If you frequently chide yourself because of your cluttered lifestyle, it signifies you are unhappy with your current situation. Your children naturally look to you for guidance, and if you send the wrong message, maintaining the home becomes a chore that everyone dreads. If you change your approach, then your children and spouse will do the same. When your family is part of the solution, the result will be a home everyone can be proud of, which also will feed your family's desire to keep your home clean and clutter-free.

Your family must contribute every day by doing something as simple as putting shoes away as soon as they are taken off. When this becomes a habit, add to it by creating another simple task, such as placing keys and cell phones in the same place every day. New habits develop only after repeated, concentrated effort, but once they are established, there is little thought involved in performing the task. The act of keeping your house clean will no longer be something your family dreads because it will become second nature to all of you.

This is true for any desired change in lifestyle. In order to lose weight, you must form new eating habits. In order to save money and get out of debt, you must create new spending habits. To raise a family that manages its own clutter, your family must form new habits. Building this type of discipline is not easy, but it is necessary to accomplish your family's goals.

As an overwhelmed parent, if the clutter in your life freezes you in your tracks and prevents you from reaching your dreams, assume it does the same for the members of your family. Free yourself and the ones you love most by allowing yourselves to flourish in your new, clutter-free environment.

About this Book

This book was written from a parent's point of view — a parent who, as a matter of fact, could never be described as a naturally neat person. For some, the need to be clean and orderly is not an inherent part of their personality. As a person grows up, gets married, and creates a family of his or her own, it becomes apparent there are many types of personalities that range from self-proclaimed "neat freaks" to "slobs" — and everything in between. Families consist of interesting blends of all of these characteristics so it is important to tolerate the behavior of others while still creating an environment where new habits can form. It may never bother your messy son that his coat is on the chair closest to the front door, yet he can still learn to place it on a hanger as soon as he enters the house. Your "neat freak" daughter may have to adjust to the idea of a taking her shoes off by the front door rather than neatly lining them up in her closet so she does not track dark footprints all through the house.

Living as a family unit requires give and take for everyone involved. Acceptance, patience, and a desire to do what is best for all members will go a long way in determining a successful outcome as you attempt to conquer the clutter that any family possesses.

The truth is that overly cluttered homes do not happen overnight but instead over a long time. Do not expect drastic changes to take place in one day or even one week; realize you must make a concentrated effort. As you learn new tricks and discover for yourself what will work for your family, you will possess the tools you need to make a permanent improvement. The pathway to improving the atmosphere and organization of your home begins with clarifying the roles of each member of your family. The process may be an uphill battle but is well worth the climb.

Charting the Way Out

This book includes a series of charts, checklists, and quizzes to help you identify what will work best for your family. Some family members may need to organize their thoughts before putting any of them into action, identifying specific thought processes in order to let go of old patterns of behavior. Each family is unique, and yours may appreciate a chart or checklist to simplify areas of your home life. There is no need to try to attempt this feat on your own when so many experts have gone on before to chart a path to success. The way out begins with reaching for help and accepting the tried and true ideas of others along the way.

Oppress the Mess Tips

Tip boxes are scattered throughout the chapters of this book, referred to as "Oppress the Mess" tips. These offer quick reminders and simple solutions that take little time but keep the mess at bay. Think of these tips as bite-sized pieces for both parents and children. Write them on sticky notes and post them on your mirrors as a different goal for each week. As your family begins to take note, your minds are being retrained and results will soon follow.

Tip #1

Oppress the Mess

Examine the ways clutter steals from you and your family.

- **Clutter wastes your valuable time** – Storing things where they are used will save your family time and frustration.

- **Clutter may cause you to waste money** – Have you ever purchased a duplicate of something you already own simply because you can no longer find the original? By eliminating clutter and realizing what you already have and where it is located, you will reduce the chances of purchasing duplicates.

- **Clutter wastes your energy** – Leaving something out of place means you adapt to it and work around it, possibly even cleaning around it. You will never be happy with the results until everything is in its place.

- **Clutter can cause accidents or bring unhealthy living conditions** – Repeatedly stepping or tripping over misplaced items on the floor is a clear signal that it is time to remove them. Growing piles of paper, magazines, or clothes invite insects and other unwelcome critters to form a home there.

One Step at a Time

This book presents a room-by-room, habit-by-habit approach to conquering the clutter in your life, making it easier to choose at least one improvement each day that will make a difference. Each step in the right direction brings success and will inspire you to proceed further down this path of remaining clutter-free.

You will find that certain chapters have information and tips you can apply immediately, while others may take longer to accomplish. The purpose of this book is to lead you to discover new ideas and embrace the fresh possibilities for your home. As you let go of past guilt or negative thinking that comes from living in an overly cluttered home, recognize these feelings may be exactly what holds you back. There is no room for blame if you hope to find the road to a better existence. What matters is that you desire better surroundings and harmony for all who enter your home, and it will require the support of your entire family to accomplish this feat.

As a parent, you may sometimes feel as if you are running through life at a full sprint, hurrying through without ever realizing why you are running that particular race in the first place. If you change your course of action and pace yourself as if you are running a marathon instead of a 100-yard dash, you will set yourself up for success. As in the story of the tortoise and the hare, a slow and steady approach will create winners out of you and your family.

With the right training, keeping an orderly home will be a side benefit to improving the teamwork and cooperation within your family. A cluttered home will no longer be your only focus, nor will it provide a constant source of shame or guilt.

Reading this book will help you learn to do the following:

- Look at your home through a fresh point of view in order to identify quick improvements.

- Establish a plan of action customized for your family and the various personalities within it.

- Find creative and fun ways to get and keep your family involved.

- Take control of the contents of your home rather than allowing them to control you.

- Set yourself up for success by focusing on small, daily improvements rather than changing your environment all at one time.

- Take the stress out of maintaining control of your home, which will open it up for the enjoyment of your family and friends.

- Develop a successful plan, even if both parents work outside the home.

- Establish a method of storing things where they are most likely to be used, which also increases the chances of them being returned to their appropriate location.

- Create ways to build fun into work days or cleaning days, making them more rewarding for the entire family.

- Dissolve the territorial attitude many kids have regarding their belongings or assigned chores; as everyone works together toward a common goal, it matters less whose job it is to do a particular task.

Chapter 1

Trapped in the Clutter Cycle

For those who are trapped in the cycle of clutter and who admit to a growing dissatisfaction with this lifestyle, you will be glad you found this book. Most likely, you find yourself in a vicious and repeating cycle, which makes you experience the following emotions:

- You become angry when other family members make a mess, leaving you to clean it up.

- Regardless of who is to blame, the messes continue to pile up around you just moments after you clean an area.

- You blame yourself for the constant presence of clutter.

- You determine that laziness is at the root of the problem, which brings guilt or frustration along with it.

- You feel as if you are the only one who cares about this problem, causing you to lose hope that the situation can ever change.

In order to help your family break out of this cycle, you must first identify the causes of your clutter. The process begins by asking some difficult questions of yourself, as well as your family:

- Does the overwhelming presence of clutter bother anyone other than me?

- Do we, as a family, want this to improve?

- How will our lives improve if we force a permanent change in this area of our lives?

- As a family, are we willing to put forth some effort on a daily basis to bring about such a change?

As you answer these questions, understand your family will adapt to the new status quo. For example, if you remove un-needed furniture to open the pathway through your living room, your kids will grow accustomed to it. If you reduce the number of books stacked on your children's bookshelves, they will soon like the look of the uncluttered shelves. So, even if your family members do not consider clutter a problem in your home, they will learn to appreciate the improvements you generate. With fewer visual distractions, they will soon adapt to the idea that less is more in your home. And, the greatest discovery of all is learning the less stuff you have, the easier it is to maintain.

Assessing Your Mess

What one person considers messy may not be such an issue to another. You may walk into a room, notice the laundry basket full of clothes and plan to get to it on the following day. Someone else may see that same basket of clothes and view it as something that needs to be taken care of immediately. A stack of unopened mail on the counter may not be a problem for your spouse, but once a stack forms, it invites more clutter. For this reason, perhaps the first thing to do as you evaluate your living conditions is to clarify exactly what you and your family consider as messy.

Once you and those in your household agree on these standards, you can better determine a healthy balance that pleases everyone. Listening to your family members' opinions of disorder and untidiness will open your eyes to what bothers them and will help you customize your plan of action for your particular family. It will demonstrate where to start as your family tackles this project together. The simple truth is if you are not a naturally neat person, your only motivation for staying on top of the clutter may be because it bothers others in your family. This is something your children need to learn as well. Keep in mind that with any family, your goal cannot be perfection. If you aim that high, you will quickly become disappointed with the results.

Another way you can customize your own plan of attack is by taking into account the geographical area and climate of your home because your challenges will differ based on what part of the country you live in. For example, if you live in Florida, you may have a problem with sand and flip-flops piling up by your front door. With extended summer months, a growing stack of pool toys or beach towels hanging over your porch railing can become a daily battle for you. On the other hand, if you live in a cold climate, such as Pennsylvania, you may find your entryway strewn with mismatched mittens or scarves, snow boots, and damp socks. As your family layers up for the colder temperatures outside, your greatest challenge might be figuring out how to keep extra sweatshirts, sweaters, and socks handy without surrendering the entrance to your home.

Your family's interests and activities are also a factor as you map your way out of an environment of clutter. If someone in your family is a musician, musical instruments might easily overtake an entire bedroom. For athletes, there will be duffle bags overflowing with shoes and gear, along with the ever-present need for clean uniforms. For dancers, a constant supply of shoes and leotards are required. Though each of these items contributes to the clutter in the home, they are also a treasured part of your family life. You must consider these factors when customizing a way to manage both the people and activities of your home.

The clutter in your home is the direct result of the people and activities that take place in and around it. Family fun centers around supporting each other through such extra-curricular activities, but if these activities also keep you traveling from sporting events to concerts to dance practices each evening, you will rarely get home before dark. If this is the case in your family, you may need to wait until your schedule lightens up before making any dramatic changes. Determine how to manage the excess equipment these activities require until you can make time to implement a permanent uncluttering strategy.

Why does this happen to us?

The Truth About Your Home and Family

Take a few minutes to examine the following statements about your family and your home. Though you may already be aware of what causes your home's clutter, it sometimes helps to see it in writing. This quick quiz may bring some truths to light that you have not yet considered.

SPECIFY TRUE OR FALSE FOR EACH STATEMENT.	TRUE	FALSE
Our family spends the majority of time at home with free leisure time.		
Whether the home is clean and uncluttered is a high priority for everyone in our family.		
Responsibilities of cleaning and maintaining the home are understood and shared among family members.		
Children, regardless of their age, have a role in maintaining the appearance of the home.		
By default, there is at least one room or space in the home that is used to store junk, making it unusable for its created purpose.		
There is at least one pet that lives within the home, even if it stays outside the majority of the time.		
Eating is allowed only in certain areas of the home.		
The items stored in each room are used in that particular room.		
The kitchen is set up so everyone can find and reach what they need in the cabinets and drawers.		
Cleaning the home is an ongoing priority so we never have to worry about embarrassment when someone drops by unannounced.		
Most members of our family would describe our home as being well organized and tidy the majority of the time.		
Most items stored in the home are used on a regular basis.		
Our car or cars fit easily into the garage.		
Number of True Answers		
Number of False Answers		

Calculate your number of true answers and number of false answers. If most of your answers are true, then you have a good system in place, as well as the support of your family to help you succeed with your goal of uncluttering the home. However, if most of your answers are false, this will help you identify why the clutter in your life seems to take over your home. Perhaps your family is rarely even home, or maybe your home is being used to store furniture for family members or future generations. Perhaps your kids acquired a collection of stray pets so it now seems as if you live in the pets' home rather than the other way around.

Regardless of why the cycle of clutter repeats itself, the time is here to change your surroundings, as well as your habits. If you retake the quiz after implementing the suggestions in this book, the goal would be for you to come up with as many true answers as possible. Though you may not have control over the amount of time your family spends at home, which is one of the questions on this quiz, most other categories are things you can gradually bring under control. Becoming aware of what needs to be done is a great starting point.

How Clutter Affects You and Your Family

Clutter does not seem to affect some personality types. In an office environment, a disorganized desk does not necessarily reflect the work of someone who is lazy or failing to meet his or her job responsibilities; on the contrary, it may reveal a person who is a vital part of the action at a workplace. As he or she quickly runs from meeting to meeting, it may be that this person rarely sits down at his or her desk to conquer the pile of paperwork that waits for him or her.

The same is true for your children. A child may be extremely organized at school but may not mind his or her room being messy at home. The clutter that surrounds the child at home may not interfere with his or her ability to focus while doing homework. He or she may lower his or her standards at home because he or she uses so much energy to keep him or herself organized in the competitive school environment.

But for other personality types, clutter does interfere with their day-to-day living. Some people cannot relax and enjoy their surroundings if their environment is untidy or unclean. They may be unable to focus on the people around them because of too much visual clutter. It goes deeper than this, though. For example, the musty smell of papers, furniture, or pet odors may adversely affect them or even their breathing, leaving them physically unable to enjoy a visit to a home like this.

As a parent, your goal is to create a home where all the personality types within your family can look forward to spending their time. You want a place where your family is proud to bring their friends. The pleasant environment of your home should be a safe haven from the pressures of the external world, and this does not happen on its own. It takes work and commitment and could require a change of attitude from your whole family.

Long-term effects on your children

The television show *Clean House*, featured on the Style Network, focuses on the severely cluttered living conditions of families around the country. By the show's 100th episode, nine families were submitted to the network by children who secretly videotaped the out-of-control environment in their homes. For additional interesting facts regarding the first 100 episodes, visit **www.mystyle.com/mystyle/shows/cleanhouse/blog/index. jsp?categoryName=clean_house&pageNum=2**.

The children in these nine particular cases saw their parents as the main reason for their clutter problem. They wanted homes they could invite their friends to instead of cringing in shame when someone asked to come inside. After numerous attempts to address the problem with their parents, these children were willing to face the embarrassment associated with being televised if it meant their home life could be different.

If children live in an environment such as this on a regular basis, it alters their behavior around other people. They may withdraw from group activities for fear they will be required to invite the group members to their own home. They may avoid sporting activities for fear their parents would not be organized enough to get them to practices or games. They may skip school because their homework or school project is not completed. In extreme cases, children learn to overly control other areas of their life, such as washing their hands repeatedly or placing too much pressure on themselves to excel in school, leading to obsessive-compulsive behaviors. If the problem of holding onto clutter develops into what is known as hoarding, the home becomes a health hazard as the piles of clutter provide places for bugs and vermin to hide. Pets may worsen the situation if not properly trained and cleaned up after, leading to unpleasant odors and an unclean and unsafe atmosphere.

Extreme cases of an overly cluttered and dirty home can destroy a family. Prolonged exposure to a worsening problem is unhealthy in every way: physically, emotionally, and socially.

Understanding and Blending Personality Types

Before you outline your plan to conquer your clutter, you need to fully understand the personality types in your family, recognizing exactly who you are dealing with. Requiring a messy person to become obsessively neat will not work. Instead, understand and work with the natural tendencies of your family members to prevent later frustration. As a parent, you should find a way to motivate each of your family members within their own personality types rather than focus all your energy on changing their behavior simply because you say it has to be done.

Your family is made up of many personality types; some are neat and others are not. Some are creative and impulsive, while others may crave structure. Some family members may have a short attention span, while others can remain focused on one project for an entire day. You need to identify what motivates each person so you can demonstrate the greatest benefit of living in an unclut-tered home that will matter most to them. Use their strengths to the advantage of the entire family. If one child likes to clean, let him or her clean, ensuring that he or she does not take on more than his or her share of the workload. If one child likes to reorganize, let him or her work through your desk drawers. For the child with a short attention span, set aside quick tasks that take less than five minutes to finish.

In a June 2007 feature segment on *60 Minutes*, Andy Rooney highlighted the marked difference in the natural tendencies regarding cleanliness and neatness between Type A and Type B personalities. A Type A personality is marked by a desire to accomplish tasks quickly and a strong need for control. A Type B personality is defined as relaxed, uncompetitive, and choosing time for self-reflection. Obviously, a person with either of these characteristics would approach the problem of clutter in very different ways. Here are some questions you can use to assess the personality types of your family members.

Cleanliness Habits of Type A/Type B Personalities

Choose the appropriate answer to identify what comes naturally for each of your family members.

1. When you first wake up each morning, you:

   A) Make the bed and hang your pajamas immediately.

   B) Leave the bed unmade and lay your pajamas on your pillow to await your arrival later that night.

2. Once you finish your shower, you:

   A) Hang your towel up to dry.

   B) Drop it on the wet floor.

3. During breakfast, you:

   A) Grab the newspaper and read the front page first.

   B) Find something to eat and search for your favorite section of the paper.

4. After you eat, you:

   A) Wash and dry your dishes and place them back in the cabinet.

   B) Pile your dishes in the sink to deal with later.

5. When getting ready for your day, you:

   A) Iron what you plan to wear, wrap the cord around the iron, and return it to its shelf.

   B) Wear your clothes wrinkled.

6. When climbing into your car for your day, you:

   A) Allow plenty of time to get to work and have a full tank of gas.

   B) Are surprised to find out you are almost out of gas and are usually running late.

7. When beginning your work day, you:

    A) Know where everything is and where to start because you straightened your desk the previous evening.

    B) Jump right into a new project, leaving the unfinished ones in piles on your desk.

8. When looking for necessary papers, you:

    A) Check your files.

    B) Check your piles.

Although this is not a scientific quiz, taking more of a humorous look at personality differences, it is easy to identify natural tendencies. This is important as you learn to recognize who plays each role within your own family. Type A personalities are able to multitask and manage many projects at once, while Type B personalities are creative and do not allow themselves to be held back by fears or anxieties. A family is a blend of all personality types, and finding ways to use the natural tendencies of each member to your advantage will simplify your path to an uncluttered lifestyle.

You may also recognize that some people are one way at work or school and may demonstrate the opposite traits at home. If someone is required to be organized at a job or at school, he or she might relax from those pressures at the end of a long day. Although this proves they like structure while at work or school, understand that they may appreciate the opportunity to take a break from it once they come home. If your family members leave a trail of backpacks, jackets, and shoes behind them, allow them to collapse on the couch, get a snack, and regroup before picking up their belongings. At that moment, listening to the details of their day takes precedence over keeping the home uncluttered.

It will take you working as a team to make this work, and, as with any successful sports team, it takes all personality types to succeed. Take a basketball team, for example. Some players are short and quick; some are steady under pressure; others are tall and great on defense; while others are great at scoring baskets. But, it takes all of them to win games and to truly remain successful throughout the long season. The same is true for you and your family.

What Lies Behind the Pattern of Clutter

As you search for what causes the pattern of clutter in your home, pay attention to the different personality types within your family. As revealed in the personality quiz in the previous section, a cluttered desk or room can be a sign of a creative person. Quickly moving from project to project, developing new ideas while enhancing older ideas, the creative person may surround himself or herself with unfinished projects in an attempt to keep the creative juices flowing the following day. Because he or she is not a naturally orderly person, leaving bits and pieces of unfinished projects on the desk may serve as a visual reminder to finish. For this reason, do not assume that clutter is automatically a result of laziness. If you always assumed that this was the problem with a particular family member, check to see if he or she is one of the creative types mentioned in the Personality Quiz. It may be that he or she needs assistance coming up with a way to manage ongoing projects. Or, perhaps he or she is too busy for his or her own good, and frequently becomes overcommitted. He or she might need your help to set boundary lines so he or she does not get in over his or her head.

But, what if laziness is what lies behind the pattern of clutter? If this is the case, be thankful because this is a correctable behavior. Children normally are on their best behavior for others and act their worst at home. Your neighbors may describe your son as the most helpful person they know, while you only see his perpetual pile of dirty clothes. These differing opinions prove your children are willing to help when they feel appreciated. If you remain consistent about what you expect from them, they will learn to follow through with their chores and will accept it as a family responsibility. However, if you clean their room for them every time it gets unbearably dirty, they will grow to expect this as well.

Begin to teach new habits, and raise the standards for what is acceptable. Provide motivation for improvement, such as a daily reward for each step your family takes. Raise awareness by showing that with a little attention every day, all tasks are much less overwhelming. If you determine your clutter is a result of the emotional ties your family members have with their belongings, be glad you recognize it now and gradually change their way of thinking. A child who is emotionally attached to his or her toys is much easier to retrain than an adult who has unintentionally fed this destructive habit for years. Begin the practice of getting rid of an old item for each new one received by anyone in the family, and emotional attachments to toys can be curtailed.

What You Tell Yourself Along the Way

What causes you hold onto unused stuff? Does it have sentimental value? Do you hope to eventually use it some day? Do you feel an amazing amount of guilt if you throw something away? Did you have to go without some necessary items during a previous period of your life, causing you to hold on to everything now?

As you wrestle with the answers to these questions, also consider what thought processes those in your family are going through. Because you are tackling this issue as a family, help your children discover these answers for themselves. If it takes you a while to figure out how your home reached its current point of clutter and whether you need to adjust your thinking for long-term improvement, the same may be true for your children.

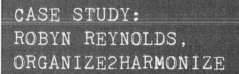

CASE STUDY: ROBYN REYNOLDS, ORGANIZE2HARMONIZE

Robyn Reynolds
Organize2Harmonize
4438 Murietta Ave. #18
Sherman Oaks, CA 91423
robynstacee@yahoo.com
http://organize2harmonize.com
310-625-6522

Organize2Harmonize, in addition to home organization, specializes in everything from estate sales to staging and coordinating moves to new locations. Robyn Reynolds, owner and proprietor of this business, says she has worked with clients who only need help with one room of their home to those who consider themselves to be hoarders. Her work with estate sales, which normally take place after the death of the property owner, allows her a front-row seat to see what those family members left behind must deal with. Testimonials from some of her clients reveal that Reynolds' cool and practical approach to estate sales provide a calm influence for both the family members and customers at the sale.

For homes with small amounts of storage space, Reynolds recommends finding furniture that serves a dual purpose, such as a trunk that can work as a coffee table or a buffet with drawers at the bottom and room for a television and stereo at the top.

The best advice Reynolds can offer to those who think they have no time to organize is to do a little at a time. And more important, once you clear off an area, even if it is a tabletop, do not allow it to become cluttered again.

"Containerize everything," Reynolds said, meaning place everything in containers. "Know where everything belongs, and make sure it is put back in place. Whether it is a bin, shelf, or cabinet, your space must work for you."

A recent client of Reynolds bragged that Organize2Harmonize provided the physical labor and organizational skills to sort through 20 years worth of stuff stacked to the ceiling in her storage room. Amazed that it only took four short hours, this client was thrilled with the results, even if it did mean that Reynolds had to coax her into letting go of many of her belongings.

Why doing nothing is still a choice

It is important to note that most people do not choose a cluttered lifestyle. Life happens, and families grow, and possessions accumulate. It was never a conscious decision to allow it to get out of control. But, choosing to do nothing will lead directly to a cluttered home. You will easily acquire more possessions than your home can hold. You must plan to rid your home permanently of hand-me-downs and unused items.

You can help your children realize this as well. Show them how cleaning their room does not happen by itself, and show them that you need their help. Many children do well with a checklist or a weekly schedule to show when things are done. Establish a day of the week for them to strip their beds and bring their bed linens to the laundry room. Set a rule that if a toy stays on the floor for a defined period, that toy is taken away for a week. Remember that you are always trying to teach them to think through these things for themselves, and it will take many kids a long time before it sinks in. But, if you make such threats and never follow through, their behavior will never change.

Recognizing your inner packrat or hoarder

Hoarding is the unhealthy action of acquiring things of little value. There is a marked difference between being a packrat and a hoarder — with hoarding falling at the extreme end of the spectrum. A hoarder is not someone who possesses well-displayed collections of dolls, cookie jars, guns, comic books, or thimbles. Hoarding is more of an unorganized and unidentified fear of throwing anything away. Hoarders end up with magazines, trash, tools, clothing, or other trinkets that intrude on their living space. At its worst, hoarding can range from having old newspapers stacked to the ceiling to filling rooms with crates full of every piece of mail ever delivered. Common sense says that if you can never find something when you need it, there is no need to keep it. But, for the hoarder, this is not a natural part of the thinking process.

The fear of needing something after it has been let go is what causes someone to hoard. They may absorb leftover items from other sources, such as garage or estate sales, and bring them into their home because it hurts them to see anything go to waste. For the hoarder, acquiring more things helps them feel better prepared for the future, and they fully intend to use everything they own. For this reason, hoarders fall into a constant cycle of obtaining new things, while the majority of their belongings remain unused. Many hoarders are lonely so they form a relationship with their stuff rather than with the people around them. However, the problem of hoarding further isolates people from their friends or family members.

Those with typical patterns of clutter are not hoarders but rather more of a packrat. A packrat can identify with many of the same thought processes a hoarder follows: holding onto items of sentimental value; saving furniture for the kids to take with them one day; and accepting hand-me-downs that are not currently needed because they hate to see them go to waste. A packrat can recognize the problem and keep it under control, limiting the harsh effects on daily living conditions. He or she may learn to work around a few stacks of magazines or newspapers but can prevent the stacks from taking over the home.

These habits of holding on to belongings worsen with age, so it is important to counteract them early on. For elderly relatives who have lived at the same place for a long time, the home serves as a museum of sorts, heralding the accomplishments and memories of all who have lived there. It is important to deprogram any thought processes that may lead to this type of behavior so such cycles do not repeat.

Keeping everything – worst case scenarios

On the A&E cable network television series *Hoarders*, the following statistics are given at the beginning of each show:

- Compulsive hoarding is a mental disorder marked by the obsessive need to keep things, even if the items are worthless, hazardous, or unsanitary.

- More than 3 million people are compulsive hoarders.

This show features the stories of some of these hoarders. There is a frequent theme behind the reason for keeping everything: The fear of needing it after it is gone. Many of the featured cases show the hoarders needing to leave their homes when others throw away the trash that has been left to collect on the floors because the act of getting rid of even worthless stuff is much too painful for them. This show demonstrates extreme cases, and it is easy to recognize the common denominators in the thinking process of each hoarder. In most instances depicted on the series, the people involved are at a breaking point with those in their lives and are either facing jail time, facing the possibility of losing custody of their children, facing eviction because of their living conditions, or are dealing with a severe health crisis. Family members who have nowhere else to turn to find help for their loved ones by submitting them to the show.

Psychologists are also involved throughout the show. They understand that for a hoarder, removing the belongings does nothing to treat the illness that lies beneath their habits. For a hoarder, throwing away their belongings is similar to depleting the stash of drugs for a drug addict: It temporarily removes the danger but does not decrease their desire or need to keep everything. They may even go through trash to rescue treasures they consider valuable. If they see a T-shirt still in good condition, even though it no longer fits anyone in the family, they feel guilt if they discard it. Plastic, refillable cups from the local corner market are considered reusable, even if they are thrown into a pile in the corner. To throw them away seems wasteful to a hoarder.

Ironically, as much as they resist any effort to change or improve their lifestyle, they hate the fact that they continue this behavior. They know it is a sickness and causes problems for the ones they love most but do not know how to fix it. Unable to meet the ultimatum given to them — which is to improve or else — many times they watch as their families move on without them. In one such case, a man referred to as Phil refused to get help until his wife finally suffered a heart attack because of the ongoing stress their living conditions caused. In another case, a woman named Patricia was unable to regain custody of her children because she could not maintain a clean and healthy lifestyle even after the television show staff cleared her home of years worth of garbage. Her husband had to leave her in order to prove to the courts that he cared about the welfare of the children, eventually obtaining sole custody of their children.

Sometimes it helps to view such extreme cases of how belongings can steal the joy from your home and your family. Allow your older children to watch an episode of a television show like this. Talk with them about the erroneous thought processes these people go through as they refuse to get rid of anything. It may provide just the motivation needed to take control of your home environment permanently. Your home is meant to be lived in and enjoyed, not to serve as a museum for past memories no matter how cherished they happen to be.

Debunking your myths – recognize false thinking as it happens

As you decide whether to keep something, throw it away, or donate it, see if you can identify any of the following thought processes as they go through your mind:

- I made this when I was younger so I want to keep it.

- We have no use for this incomplete set of dishes, but I want to keep them in the family because they belonged to Granny.

- I got a good deal on that so I hate to get rid of it.

- We have no place to keep books, but they are good collector's items.

- We already have several of these items somewhere, but because I cannot find them, we will purchase more.

- When we refinish the basement, we will need additional furniture or electronics for that area so we need to keep these items until then.

- We are updating the decorations in this particular room, but the old ones are still good. We will just hang onto these paintings and curtains for later because someone will use them.

- Because we do not know what to do with this stuff, we will just move it to the attic/basement until we have time to go through it.

- Old sports uniforms and dance and cheer costumes are so much of our kids' past that we can just keep those items hanging in their closets to remind them of the fun times they used to have.

- Though we do not need this now, someone in the family may be able to use it in the future.

If this is what you or your family members think, recognize it as a myth, and retrain your mind to embrace healthier options rather than making the choice to keep everything. Keep it, throw it away, recycle it, or donate it; these are your only four choices for items if your goal is to unclutter your home. If you decide to keep it, it must have a home, or you must have a logical plan on where to store it. Placing it in a plastic bin in the attic or basement because you are not quite ready to get rid of it will only create more work for you later. As you minimize your belongings, keeping your home uncluttered will take care of itself.

Remove Your Obstacles

Taking a step back to examine your situation with fresh eyes will help you clearly determine the obstacles ahead of you. The barriers that prevent you from breaking the pattern of behavior may be as unique as each family member. The hurdles present in your personal obstacle course will vary so the first step is to identify exactly what stands in your way.

The obstacles you find on your uncluttering course may be some of the following:

- You may have too many people living in a very small space.

- Your busy schedules do not allow any time for cleaning or maintaining your home.

- Your garage is being used to store someone's belongings so you can no longer use it as it was intended.

- You lack storage space.

- If you are home schooling or work from home, the necessary equipment may take over the rest of your living areas.

- The thought of cleaning your home is overwhelming, and because you know it will take several days, you put it off as long as possible.

- It takes so much effort to clean your home and so little effort for it to become cluttered you begin to ask why you should bother.

- Your home is cramped with too much furniture so it feels overcrowded.

- Some items in your home are never used so they take up space and invite more clutter.

Rediscover Your Dignity

Most likely, the biggest change that needs to take place in your own journey from clutter to clarity is within your mind. Underneath your piles of clutter, you will rediscover your own dignity and believe you and your loved ones deserve better than this. Eliminate "less than" thinking, and eliminate referring to yourself or your family in a negative light, as if you deserve less than the best. Allow yourself to shake off the thinking that tries to hold you down and prevents you from a lasting home improvement.

Part of this process may include disposing of any items that cause you shame or embarrassment. If you wear clothing with small stains you hope no one notices, get rid of it. Items with holes, clothes pinned together, or items with missing buttons should either be repaired or replaced. Socks that do not match should never be worn together. You may be asking yourself, why does it matter? It matters because you deserve better, and so does your family. Once you remove the items that bring you shame, it will be easier to rise above these obstacles. All improvements to your lifestyle begin and end with the mind so show yourself that you are serious, and give yourself a reason to rediscover your dignity.

To start, have a big "We are better than this" party in your living room. Form a pile in the center of the room of anything that needs repair: If it has holes, is missing a button, or is ripped, too tight, too short, or too long, put it in the pile. If it causes someone in your family to feel self-conscious by wearing it, throw it in the pile. This includes any towels, sheets, and blankets with holes or rips. Add to the pile any shoes that are cracked on the bottom or have holes in them. Any belts that are ripping through from wear and tear, add to the pile.

Engaging in this activity sends the message to your kids that they do not need to keep things that no longer work for them. Shoes are not meant to last forever and neither are belts, coats, or other clothing items. So why keep them? Your family may need this reminder from you and permission to do something about it.

You can then determine if any of these items are worth repairing. If they were repaired, would they honestly be worn again? If not, throw them away or donate them to a charity that will repair and reuse them. This activity alone will go a long way to de-cluttering your family's closets and dressers. Immediately take those items in your pile that are damaged beyond repair, and place them in a trash bag. Remove them from your home, and your family will begin to get the message that they deserve better. They will rediscover their own dignity through the process. As you emphasize that your family deserves the best, they will soon begin to believe you, and you may find you no longer miss any of the old items.

Chapter 2

When Your Stuff Owns You

W hen a couple first begins their life together, they may rent a tiny apartment, furnish it with second-hand furniture, and fill their cupboards with treasured wedding gifts. There are few belongings, but few are needed to find happiness. With a tight budget, they make due without many of the "must haves" in today's society. The couple enjoys a simple way of life, and with a pared down lifestyle, it is much easier to maintain control of their home and its clutter.

As time goes on, the couple upgrades to nicer cars, new furniture, big screen televisions, and electronic accessories, such as speakers, game systems, and stereo equipment. They start a family, and the items required to take care of a baby quickly fill their home. This growing family moves to a larger house with a big yard, and they trade in for a larger vehicle. With a bigger home comes more furniture, decorations, and belongings. Increasing the number of bathrooms and bedrooms equals additional towels and bed linens, and with the yard, a lawn mower and yard equipment soon follows. In a matter of just a few years, the amount of objects this couple owns has multiplied at an amazing pace.

Assume the pattern continues and the couple has another child or two. The kids grow up and beg for a pet, begin to play sports, and get their first bicycle, complete with a helmet and elbow pads. The younger children acquire their own toys, and the movie and video game collection takes over the family room. A couple home computers are stashed wherever possible. Soon the kids are all in school or pre-school, bringing home a daily supply of papers, crafts, and poems written just for their mother or father, all of which are priceless. The first science project is soon due, requiring a model volcano or village mounted on a massive cardboard platform that takes over the kitchen table. After the two weeks of effort invested in the project, no one wants to see it thrown away.

Within a ten-year span, the simple lifestyle this couple began with is unrecognizable. They outgrow their home, as well as their vehicles. As they acquire new pieces of furniture, they hang on to the older pieces in case a friend or future family member will need it. Examining this household 25 years into the marriage, you find a house full of treasured memories, keepsakes, photos, trophies, and more. Life, by its very existence, brings with it many belongings. It unknowingly happens: Your stuff multiplies and takes over open space in your home, garage, basement, or attic. That is, unless you have a plan of action on how to deal with it.

It is safe to assume that the longer you live in your home, the more your belongings will multiply, becoming a factor in managing your household. Do not yield to the increase of possessions that longs to take over your home. Do not spend your treasured free time stepping over belongings that are no longer in use. Your stuff does not own the home; either control your belongings, or they will control you. You need to establish an ongoing way to filter out the old before you bring in the new.

Obeying Your Stuff

The more stuff you own, the time, money, and energy needed to care for it increases. Buying a boat requires you to insure it, clean it, protect it from the elements, transport it, and even find a place to dock it on the waterfront. Your plans for that boat may be well worth this type of effort as you envision you and your family skimming across the water at sunset. The thrill of owning your own boat is diminished, however, as you realize you may need to pay additional money to store it during the off season. Finally, as you clean it on a monthly basis, you realize your weekends are spent doing everything the boat tells you. As you weigh the number of times you actually enjoy it during the warm summer months, you have to determine if it is worth what it requires of you throughout the year.

Could it be your boat ends up owning you rather than you owning it? If so, this motivates you to take action quickly and resolve the problem. If you determine that your boat purchase requires more work and expense than enjoyment, it may be time to sell it.

Extreme Cases of Hoarding

Chapter 1 discussed hoarding to some extent, but the repercussions of hoarding deserve additional attention because these are truly horror stories. Keep in mind that the act of hoarding is a sign of an obsessive compulsive disorder, which requires ongoing treatment as a form of a mental illness. According to The International Obsessive Compulsive Disorder Foundation, which can be found online at **www.ocfoundation.org**, the initial onset of hoarding symptoms occurs in children or adolescents. Though not a disorder at this early age, the behavior manifests and progresses with time. In order to treat the external symptoms of refusing to get rid of things, the disorganized thought processes and internal fear of letting go must be addressed. The following stories are some of the most extreme cases, but they easily emphasize the curse of too many belongings.

- According to the MSNBC.com article, "Engulfed in Clutter, Hoarders Keep Heaping It On," a 62-year-old woman from Shelton, Wash., suffocated under a pile of clothing in January 2006. Later reports confirm the pile of debris pinned her while she searched for a lost telephone.

- *The Times Union* reports of two recent "deaths by hoarding" in Great Britain. One report describes a man who literally burrowed through a ceiling high trash pile in his home. He got lost in the tunnels and died of thirst. In another instance, a 3-foot pile of unopened packages, as well as clothing, suitcases, and electronics, crushed a woman when they fell on her.

How Much Stuff or Clutter Can You Afford?

Although the previous examples are extreme, here are some everyday ways clutter may cost your family:

- According to the National Soap and Detergent Association, removing clutter would eliminate 40 percent of housework in the average home because the act of cleaning the home is magnified by all that is found within it. If you have too much stuff, much of your time cleaning is spent relocating items from one place to another.

- Americans spend 55 minutes a day, or roughly 12 weeks a year, looking for items they know they own but cannot find, according to a Boston marketing firm.

- Harris Interactive, a market research firm, reports that 23 percent of adults say they pay bills late (and incur fees) because they lose the notices.

You must ask yourself a few questions to determine what your clutter is truly costing you in time, wasted energy, money, and even your relationships.

- Is it easy to play the out-of-sight, out-of-mind game and ignore the excess because you found another place to store it?

- As the weekend approaches, do you look for ways to avoid being home because you find the mess too overwhelming to try to bring under control?

- Do you feel you need a larger place to live strictly because you need more room for your belongings?

- Are you able to use your home as you intended when it was first purchased or leased?

- Do your family members feel ashamed to invite friends over?

- Do you feel overwhelmed and burdened when you are alone in your home?

- Do you desire a home that provides peace and harmony to all who enter?

If the answer to any of these questions is yes, then draw your own line in the sand to determine what you are willing to accept as too much clutter. Any amount of clutter that steals your joy, affects the use of your home, and causes stress is too much clutter. Do not give clutter more power than it deserves. If it infringes on your lifestyle, as well as the lifestyle of your family and the atmosphere of your home, it is time to eliminate the clutter, once and for all.

Storage Industry Insanity

As you examine the question of how much clutter you can afford, consider the boom of the self-storage industry across the United States. These statistics alone reflect the idea that Americans fall victim to their belongings owning them.

- According to the Self Storage Association, it took the industry more than 25 years to build its first billion square feet of space; it added the second billion square feet in just eight years (from 1998 to 2005).

- In 1984, there were 6,601 storage facilities offering 290 million square feet of space. By the end of 2009, there were 46,000 facilities representing 2.21 billion square feet.

- Currently, one out of every ten households rent a storage facility to house their extra stuff, an increase from one in 17 households in 1995.

- The gross revenue for the self storage industry in 2009 was $22 billion.

Ironically, the size of our houses increased in direct proportion to these figures. In 1975, the average size of a house in America was 1,675 square feet. By 2005, the average size climbed to 2,434 square feet — an increase in size of more than 45 percent. Even though the average house increased in the size of living space, the need for additional storage space continued to rise.

This draws attention to the fact that Americans, in general, are infatuated with consumerism, which is defined as the desire to purchase goods in ever greater amounts or larger sizes. In other words, the larger the homes, the more Americans purchase to fill them, but the amount of stuff is still outgrowing the size of homes. At an average cost of $125 per month, a 10-foot by 15-foot unit can be rented, which stores three full rooms worth of furniture, and many families rent more than one unit.

Storage units may be initially viewed as short-term solutions — as a way to temporarily store excess belongings during a move or until the items can be sorted and discarded or sold. But, many times, items are left for years in storage units with rising costs that can cripple the owner financially if he or she does not have a predetermined plan on how to deal with belongings permanently.

You must ask yourself if it is worth it in the end before considering self-storage as a short-term solution. If your home is in the process of a remodeling, it could be a way of temporarily removing the large items from the home. However, if your remodel work is complete and you have no desire to return those items to your home, take that as a sign to get rid of the stored items. If you use a storage unit for a move to a new home and leave boxes of items in storage that you do not need on a regular basis, discard, sell, or donate those items. Try to think long term, and do not allow yourself to fall into the trap of storing items away from the home. You are essentially paying rent so your belongings will have a place to stay so do not pay to store worthless junk. You must determine if you own your stuff or if your stuff owns you.

Storage unit lessons learned

You do not have to search hard to find storage unit stories about the curse of too many belongings and lessons learned the hard way. For example:

- Max Wong, a contributor to the website Wisebread: Living Large on a Small Budget, found at **www.wisebread. com**, reported the story of a friend named Sarah. Sarah was a single parent who quit her job to be a stay-at-home mom to her newly adopted daughter. She spread her valuable furniture out over four individual storage units at a cost of $200 per month, per unit. Sarah's intentions were to sell some of the items, while saving those that carried the most value to her. However, as her pace of life quickened with the arrival of her daughter, her storage situation soon spun out of control. Over five years, she invested $48,000 into storing her furniture. The end result was that she fell behind in her home mortgage because of the expense and was still forced to sell all of her stored furniture because she could no longer afford to store it.

- Marianne Giullian, a contributor for the website Dollar Stretcher, which can be found at **www.stretcher.com/ index.cfm**, shares the story of a friend who paid $100 per month for a storage unit for a 15-year period. She finally moved but ran out of time to go through her belongings. After paying a total of $18,000 in rent, all items were eventually donated to Goodwill.

- Despite the recent economic downturn, the storage industry is booming in what they refer to as "foreclosures." As written in many contracts offered by various storage companies, if you rent a unit and fall behind on payments, you are essentially locked out of your unit. The storage companies send a notice, normally providing 30 days to respond, and if you fail to respond, the storage companies then auction off the entire contents of your unit to the highest bidder. The entire contents of some units are sold for a total of $5. Not only do you end up losing all of your possessions, but you are also charged for the cost of the auction as well.

- Laura Leigh Fields shares a vivid story of the exact scenario mentioned before on **www.helium.com/items/852236-reflections-losing-a-storage-unit**. After paying the deposit on her storage unit and moving in all of her belongings because of a temporary relocation, she entered the hospital for a scheduled surgery and was shocked to receive notice that she fell behind on her storage unit payment just three weeks after renting the unit. She later found out that she paid the deposit only rather than the first month's rent. Being short on funds, she went to remove her items from the unit, but the lock was already changed on her unit. The contents were auctioned off for a total of $35 just a few days later, not even a month after she signed the contract.

The Shopping Epidemic

As you examine the reasons behind the curse of your clutter and find difficult answers to the question of how much stuff you can actually afford, you must also examine the shopping habits of those in your family. As your kids grow older, if you detect they have problems impulse shopping or have to buy something every time they go into a store, whether it is needed or not, it is time to intervene as a parent. You must curb impulse shopping for yourself as well so you can control what new items enter the home. Only buy what you need and what you have room to store. You may need to set guidelines for new purchases of clothing, toys, kitchen appliances, or even furniture.

For example, what if you set a rule that states for every new item brought into the home, two similar items must be removed to create additional room? Would this help your children evaluate whether they really need to buy a new toy, knowing they must give up two toys in order to make room for the new toy? Is a new cooking appliance necessary for a kitchen already filled with shiny appliances? Could this new system work for purchasing new clothing as well?

The point is that many people fall into the habit of buying something simply because they find a good deal. An example of this is clothing that hangs unused in a spare closet for months or years with tags proudly displaying drastically reduced prices. Children are naturally impulse buyers, falling victim to the marketing schemes of retailers. Saturday morning advertisements fill their minds with numerous items they can no longer live without, and simply entering a store requires them to walk past the latest models of swing sets, bicycles, and children's swimming pools. Guarding your family against such pitfalls will help them control their spending, as well as prevent excess clutter from invading your home.

The truth is many who have a problem with clutter also have a problem with shopping. Because shopping just for the sake of shopping can be an addiction in and of itself, here are a few warning signs to decide if shopping is getting out of hand:

- Does the shopper shop several times a week, buying something on each trip?

- Does the shopper hide his or her purchases or receipts, covering up how much he or she spent?

- Does the shopper tend to spend money he or she does not really have, using credit cards with no way to pay?

- Does the shopper purchase frequently online or from the shopping network channels on television?

- Does the shopper use shopping to improve his or her mood or to escape depression?

- Does the shopper purchase an increasing number of unneeded items that remain untouched afterward?

If the answer to any of these questions is yes, then it is time to get these shopping habits under control. It is imperative you set shopping guidelines for all members of your family and stick to them. A family requires frequent trips to the store, but be aware of the habits your children pick up at an early age. If left unmanaged, these habits are difficult to overcome as adults. Teaching children early on to control their spending, as well as how to manage their belongings, will benefit them as they grow older and start their own families.

In order to curb impulse shopping, follow these guidelines:

1. Recognize the problem and establish accountability to someone to answer for this behavior. If you are the culprit, do not shop alone. If it is one of your family members, give them a budget before they go shopping, and make sure they stick to it.

2. Pay with cash for everything. The best part about cash is that once it is gone, it is gone. Overspending is no longer an option.

3. Set a budget for all shopping trips. As a parent, you know how much groceries cost for the week so stick to that number. Use coupons and save money.

4. Avoid going to superstores if you only need groceries so you do not pick up other items while there.

5. Plan a shopping list in advance. *See Chapter 14 for more information on this topic.*

6. Be aware of marketing schemes in advance, and teach your children about them. The items placed along the checkout lines are geared for impulse buyers. Have frequent "What are they trying to sell us and why?" conversations with your children. Have these conversations following television commercials.

7. Wait before purchasing an item. Take a week, and if you still feel as strongly about it, then choose what you will give up in order to make room for that new item if you do choose to buy it.

To purchase or not to purchase?

When making the decision to purchase something and bring a new item into the home, consider the following tips offered by Lorie Marrero, certified professional organizer, author, and president of a company called The Clutter Diet®. The Clutter Diet is an online support company that teams families with professional organizers. Marrero offers the following tips to consider before purchasing any new item.

O p p r e s s   t h e   M e s s

Tip #2

Don't Let Clutter in the Door!

Prevent clutter by asking these five questions before buying a new item:

1. Who owns this already and might share it with me?

2. What do I already have that is like this?

3. Where will this be stored?

4. When will I have time to use it and maintain it?

5. Why do I want to buy this?

Courtesy of **www.clutterdiet.com**

Following these guidelines for clothing, furniture, and home goods will drastically change your thought process before buying any new item. Fewer purchases translate easily to less clutter.

Giving Yourself Permission to Change

You now recognize the behaviors of the past, identifying the obstacles of too many belongings, lack of time and/or space, and the habits of your own family members. The one thing that must be addressed before you are free to move forward is the battle that takes place within yourself. If you frequently blame yourself or refer to yourself as lazy and undisciplined, you have to put a stop to this habit. The truth is that all change begins in the mind, and you will never move forward until you release yourself from the past and give you and your family permission to change. Never be your own worst enemy.

Focus your energy on moving forward, opening your mind to the home you foresee for your family. It will never happen on its own, nor can it happen if you hold on to your past. Just like your boxes of unused items, it may be time to let go and discard your old way of thinking.

In the next chapter, you will sharpen your focus on ways to keep your family involved in the uncluttering process. Your battle to an uncluttered home should not pit you against your family. You will only find success if this is a common goal among your family members so outlining the benefits for everyone is an important first step.

Chapter 3

A Family Affair —
Setting Yours Up
for Success

Y ou cannot change your home environment on your own. But, before leading your family down this new path, you may need to first change your entire attitude toward housecleaning and uncluttering your home. If you dread these tasks yourself so will your children. If you criticize and redo everything after they have done it, they will lose the incentive to try. If you present your home's clutter as a huge problem and something to be ashamed of, your family may feel you are overreacting. Instead, stay motivated and pleasant. If you display a new attitude toward your home and your family, it will become contagious.

Next, you must recognize you need the support of your family, requiring a commitment from each member. If you detect signs that your children demonstrate the need to keep everything, the best time to address this behavior is when they are young. You may have to decide for them which items they should keep or discard until they can think it through for themselves. You may need to remove unused items when your children are not present. With some children, "out of sight, out of mind" holds true.

Other children will show an emotional attachment to their belongings. Help them work through the process of how they will take care of any new items. Establish rules to govern their belongings so they are not overwhelmed at an early age. For example, if your kids receive a new toy as a gift, have them remove one old toy from their room. They could take this used toy and donate it to a children's shelter or another organization. Teach them that downsizing on their own will give them more time to enjoy their belongings because they will spend less time cleaning and more time playing.

Parent versus Drill Sergeant

Sometimes it may seem you as a parent are responsible for every action your kids make. Try not to think of the atmosphere in your home in this way because it places too much pressure on you and establishes you as the role of drill sergeant. Your true goal is for your kids to improve their own habits and organizational skills rather than having to nag them on a daily basis or taking on all cleaning duties yourself. Take yourself out of the drill sergeant role as often as possible by establishing the rules and allowing the rules to speak for you.

Getting the Family to Buy In

You may already sense that any commitment to change must begin with a family meeting. Before this takes place, it is important for you and your spouse to agree on how to present these ideas to your children. You cannot treat your spouse as if he or she is one of the children, and you need to present a unified front before addressing your children. If your spouse is typically unwilling to assist in the maintenance of the home, deal with these issues privately. Make sure your spouse understands you need him or her to join you in creating a sense of excitement. If you are successful, the more the children learn to do on their own, the more pleasant the home will be for everyone to enjoy.

Rather than dreading the family meeting, create an event that is something to look forward to for each child. Order pizza or bake a special dessert. Do not allow it to be a painful confrontation where everyone is referred to as sloppy and made to feel ashamed. Do not allow anyone to be put down or criticized during the meeting, and do not play the blame game.

Explain to your family you want to remove yourself from the "Inspector" or "supervisor" position. Remind them that you hate having to nag them to get things done as much as they hate being on the receiving end of the nagging. Steer them in a specific direction, but invite them to be a part of the solution to improve the home environment and to take pride in their efforts. Once they understand how an uncluttered home will benefit each person, your children will be more likely to contribute in a positive way. The first step to ensure your family members are willing to contribute to your goals of uncluttering the home is to make sure they are well informed and engaged in your new lifestyle choice.

Running your family meeting

Start by asking each member of your family to name something he or she can do on a daily basis to make a difference. If they form their own ideas, they are more likely to follow with genuine effort so encourage their input. It may be something as simple as picking up trash or unneeded papers and throwing them away before they go to bed each night. Emphasize that the endeavor to unclutter the home is not a one-day task, but instead, it requires their attention over a long time.

It is also important to take it one step at a time. Set measurable goals so you can celebrate when you see obvious progress. Initial success breeds additional success; set goals that conquer several tasks at one time. For example, if your goal is to vacuum your floors on a weekly basis, then the floors must be free of clutter. Create a chart that lists your goals on one side and the ways you will reward your family on the other. Appreciate your progress, and it will continue, possibly even surpassing your original goals.

Follow the Disney model

Before your family balks at this idea of teamwork and the difference it can make, share with them the story of Walt Disney and his requirement for the entire staff at each of his theme parks. Both Walt Disney World® and Disneyland® are known for being impeccably clean, which leads the millions of guests the parks entertain each year to think before they litter. Of course there are certain "cast members" — park staff — required to sweep and take out trash as part of their daily job. But, if a stray piece of trash or leftover food finds its way to the ground, do not be surprised if Mickey Mouse himself picks up the trash. Every Disney employee is required to correct a problem if they see it. Walt Disney understood that a clean environment breeds a clean environment. This means that when the daily guests notice how clean their surroundings are, most people will naturally do their part to help keep it clean. This same approach can work for your family as well. Once your family members grow accustomed to living in a tidy and uncluttered environment, they will soon invest their efforts into keeping it that way.

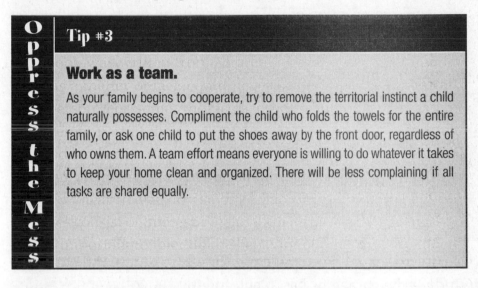

Tip #3

Work as a team.

As your family begins to cooperate, try to remove the territorial instinct a child naturally possesses. Compliment the child who folds the towels for the entire family, or ask one child to put the shoes away by the front door, regardless of who owns them. A team effort means everyone is willing to do whatever it takes to keep your home clean and organized. There will be less complaining if all tasks are shared equally.

Creating a mission statement for each room of your home

The next thing you should do in your family meeting is to get everyone to fill in the blank for the following question:

I want a home that _____.

An example of a typical response could be:

I want a home that is welcoming, fun to be in, and a place to invite our family and friends on a regular basis.

Depending on the age of your children, you will get varying responses to this question. You may want to list your family's responses on a white board, allowing everyone to see the answers.

Restate their ideas as you write them, giving value to the input of each family member. Once every family member goes through this process, they will begin to realize they have a role in creating the home they desire. This should be the case regardless of the age of your children. You gradually remove the idea that it is up to you as the parent to be the only one responsible for the appearance and organization of the home; you can teach your children better organizational skills.

Before your meeting is complete, you will need to form a mission statement for your home. Your mission statement should be comprised of the answers your family members provided for what they want the home to be. For example, it could read like this:

The Smith Family will have a home that is open to friends, that provides love and laughter, and that is a home of peace and comfort. Our home will be a place where great memories are created for all who enter.

Next, create a mission statement for each room in the home, including the garage or basement. Identify how the entire family wants the living room used. Allow each child to state the purpose of his or her own bedroom. You and your spouse should outline the purpose of your own room as well, making sure you understand what the other has in mind. The mission statements will prevent a particular room from being used as a "junk room" by default, and the process of filtering out what does not belong will become much easier when measured against the purpose of each room.

This family meeting and completing your mission statements are vital first steps in removing any negative connotations that come with the idea of cleaning the house. It is where you state your common goals and spread out the responsibilities to everyone. By opening the doors to communication and allowing everyone to express their ideas, you are inviting them to become part of the team. And, you will depend on this teamwork to propel you further down this path to a clutter-free home.

A Six-week Commitment

Now that you have your family's attention, it is time to ask them for a commitment to accomplish these goals together. As with any new resolution, you want to avoid the typical let down that follows if you do not find immediate success. You can avoid this trap by asking first for a six-week commitment. Your six-week commitment asks members of your family to make a change for the next six weeks. Studies show that any new habit is formed after it is done for 30 days so your goal in asking for six weeks allows a little wiggle room at the beginning of this trial period. Getting a firm commitment for a six-week time frame should seem manageable and provides a great platform for your family to begin this journey. There will be good days and bad days, but you are seeking a marked improvement over this six-week period.

At the same time, keep your long-term goals in sight. You desire a change of lifestyle for your family — not just six weeks worth of improvement. Those who succeed in reaching their goals are those who change their habits along with their way of thinking. Still, your family may balk if you rush in with your drastic ideas for improvement so break into bite-sized pieces. Celebrate the small victories, and soon they will snowball into much bigger accomplishments. Your family may never realize it, but you are teaching them to be self-disciplined, which is a trait they will never outgrow.

Go ahead and set a series of weekly meetings during this six-week period, choosing a regular meeting time. Discuss what is working well and what is not. Allow your kids to take turns running the meetings. Copy your list of tasks that each person can do on a daily basis and post it somewhere in your home so everyone in your family can see it. Keep your white board free to be used for the following meetings. Use your momentum to build on your success from week to week.

Before your kick-off meeting ends, choose a date that your family refers to as "Cleaning Day." Choose a date with no scheduled activities, ensuring there are no interruptions from computers, cell phones, or visiting friends. Choose a charity, preferably one that means something to everyone in your family, to receive your donations at the end of the day. It might be wise to schedule cleaning day for the day before trash is collected so that all items you discard can be taken directly to the curb. Allow your family members to choose which area of the home they want to work in, or set up teams of two to tackle projects together.

The initial cleaning day

Get plenty of cleaning supplies before your scheduled cleaning day. Divide them into baskets so each child has what he or she needs handy. Keep the focus of this day on the inside of the home, allowing other days to be focused on the yard area.

Try some of the following to add pizzazz to your cleaning day:

- Allow children to work together on their rooms, but give them a time limit for each one so they do not drag the process out as long as possible.

- Assign a chore to each person, regardless of what room the chore takes place in. Have one child remove all the bedding and start washing it. Have another child pick up all the dirty clothes on the floor. Someone else can do the dishes and put them back in their proper place. Someone can sweep and mop all floors, while another person is in charge of vacuuming. It feels less overwhelming and allows everyone to move at his or her own pace.

- Play loud and fun music and set a two-hour time limit to race against the clock. See who can make the most progress during this time. Establish a reward, such as having a friend over to spend the night or choosing a restaurant for the next family outing for the person who makes the most progress in two hours.

- Scale down the number of toys, books, or clothing your children own by determining a reward for whoever comes up with the most items to donate to charity.

- Take before and after photos to show your progress.

- Assign a child who is well organized to sort through your junk drawers. Buy a few sorting trays, and they will soon have a system they are extremely proud of that works well for everyone else. Allow them to temporarily label each drawer with a sticky note or label that identifies the contents of each drawer by category so everyone else will understand the new system.

Maintaining your momentum

So, what happens after your initial cleaning day? Focus on creating simple, daily habits so they become permanent. Consider some of the following ideas:

- Make each trip to another room count for something. When using the restroom, place all dirty clothes in the hamper. If walking through the kitchen, throw away any trash you see on the counters.

• Teach your kids to take something with them, such as shoes, backpacks, or toys, if they are heading to their bedrooms for another reason.

• Set items in a basket at the foot of the stairs that need to be taken up on the next trip up.

• Gather contents from all garbage cans at once before taking it to the curb on pick-up day.

• Clear counters and tables before leaving a room at night.

• Think of small, two-minute jobs that can be done quickly and between other activities. For example, clean your sliding glass doors with a glass wipe while letting the dog out, or dust the mantel when a commercial comes on television.

With your long-term goal in mind, begin each week with a house that is in order and commit to returning it to that state before the next week begins. Compliment your children for what they do without being asked. Write thank you notes on their mirrors to surprise them. Ask them for ideas on how to store their own stuff. When it gets tough to continue, be honest with them about how you are also struggling to create new habits. Be sure to offer your family praise about how much improvement you have already noticed.

Rewarding your family

Determine something that benefits the entire family as a reward at the end of the six-week period. Throw a pizza party for friends and family in your newly uncluttered home. You may plan a weekend trip away with just the family. Perhaps they would enjoy a picnic in the park with a nice bike ride at the end of the day. You can also consider purchasing an item for the home that the entire family can use. Give them a reason to pull together and think of themselves as a team. This will allow them to provide encouragement for each other as you begin this journey. Your family's success depends on everyone, and the more they understand that, the easier it will be to travel this road together.

Why it matters

As you plan your new strategy to unclutter your home, recognize that your most important goal is to present the idea to your family that an uncluttered environment matters to each of them in his or her own way. You know your family so figure out why an uncluttered home is significant to each individual. You may have a daughter that hates being late so help her understand why staying organized will take the pressure off when it is time to walk out the door. Your son may like to sleep as late as possible, so open his eyes to the idea that he can sleep in if he prepares for school as much as possible in advance by choosing his clothes the night before, packing his backpack, and packing his lunch for the next day. Your spouse may long for a weekend not filled with household chores, so offer to help throughout the week so he or she may truly get a weekend free from housework.

Supervisors at any workplace will tell you they get better results from their employees when they inspire them to improve rather than tearing them down or criticizing every move — and the same is true for your family. It is not necessary to spend time complaining about the past and how much you hate the current way of life in your home. Focus on the overall improvements that take place, and help your family do the same. As you raise the standard one step at a time, your family will adjust, and your home will reap the benefits. You may need to remind yourself that you are not trying to get them to perform to your standards — you are trying to get them to raise their own.

Fighting the urge to do it all yourself

One last warning before you move to the next phase of uncluttering your home: You must fight the urge to do it all yourself. You may be a perfectionist, believing you do a better job on your dishes or laundry than anyone else in your family. But, the members of your family will never learn if you do not allow them to try. Keep in mind that even doing chores needs to be fun, and fun does not mean having a parent stand over you, expressing his or her disgust because your work is not up to par. Does it really matter if your son misses a spot while vacuuming the floor? You may need to re-evaluate your standards as you learn to delegate and teach others how to help. As long as your kids view a parent as the only caretaker of the home, the atmosphere will never truly change.

Many parents enjoy cleaning only when everyone else is out of the house, but your family will never buy into the concept that this is a team effort if they come home to a clean house without ever becoming a part of the solution. It is in their best interest to learn to correct a cluttered area on their own. They must learn to do laundry, clean dishes, take out the trash, and clean the bathroom — or their cluttered lifestyle will follow them into adulthood.

The next chapter will examine the natural clutter zones that intrude into each home. By setting up your home in a way that works best for your family, you can easily overcome these issues.

CASE STUDY:
SHARON McRILL,
THE BETTY BRIGADE

Sharon McRill
The Betty Brigade
1901 Sunrise St.
Ann Arbor, MI 48103
service@bettybrigade.com
www.bettybrigade.com
888-74-BETTY (888-742-3889)

It was a layoff from her corporate marketing career at a popular national bookstore chain that spurred Sharon McRill to open her own business in

2003. Since then, she has served 800 clients, working side by side with them to make a difference in their own homes.

"The entire time I was working, I kept thinking how much I needed an assistant to keep my home life under control," she explains. Now, The Betty Brigade is a true brigade, boasting six staff members and two offices. McRill finds herself frequently hired by families to help their older parents whose houses are filled with a lifetime of stuff. Though the clients find it overwhelming, The Betty Brigade can conquer a large project by working in several rooms at once.

Word of mouth and references from probate attorneys brings The Betty Brigade business with older clients from the greater Detroit area. She even speaks now on the topic of preparing elderly adults for downsizing and moving into assisted living homes. When uncluttering such homes, McRill has rediscovered everything from an envelope holding five loose diamonds to lost stock certificates to savings bonds.

McRill frequently calls on appraisers to determine what holds value and what is junk. She goes through each item with her client before it gets packed away to be transported to a new home. Some items go to resale shops, with the additional income reinvested into the home. Some are donated to local charities. She takes all papers to an off-site shredder service at the end of a completed project.

The largest obstacle to getting organized and uncluttering the home that McRill sees on a regular basis is that families "overbook" themselves by running from activity to activity with no quiet time to spend at home. For busy families, disorganization is not an option because they lose so much time looking for things they cannot find. By prioritizing, setting boundaries, and delegating tasks, any family can learn to be organized.

"We find that people are overwhelmed by their stuff and don't know where to begin so we save a family time, energy, and money. By bringing in a large team, we can accomplish quite a bit in a short period of time. But, above all else, we remove the frustration of living in disorganization so they find hope. We offer our clients a maintenance program so they can keep it going on their own."

Chapter 4

Conquering Your Clutter Zones

Now that you have examined the varied personality types of your family members and outlined a plan of action, it is time to identify your clutter zones. Like a magnet, unused items are drawn to cluttered areas. By keeping these zones free of clutter, your family will function better and your home atmosphere will improve. Your family will learn that shoes go on the shoe rack instead of on the floor and will know where important papers need to go in order to get them signed. They will notice dirty dishes stacked up where they do not belong and make an effort to clean them and store them in their proper places.

Uncluttering Your Home as if Placing it on the Market

Have you ever visited a model home in a new subdivision? It provides an inviting scenario with warm colors that beckon visitors to come inside. Each room has a well-defined purpose, housing only items that serve that room's purpose. Closets contain minimal belongings, and the walls are covered with just enough decoration, never overly cluttered. Shelves house only a few trinkets that are pleasing to the eye. There is no evidence of any house pets. The exterior of the home is well lit, and the entrance is enhanced by landscaping that does not overpower or cover up the home. The welcoming environment allows families to easily picture themselves living there, being successful, happy, healthy, and using each room to its fullest.

Think for a moment about what is missing from the model home: Toys, shoes, or yard tools do not block the entrance. The laundry room is used only for laundry, and the countertops and tabletops are not stacked with items that belong elsewhere. Dining room tables are free to serve meals.

As you learn to look at your home through fresh eyes, try to picture it as a model home and ask yourself these questions:

1. Is the purpose for each room well defined and is the room outfitted for that purpose?

2. Are the walkways through each room clear, creating open and inviting spaces?

3. Are the walls visually cluttered?

4. Is there plenty of outside light coming in through the windows, instantly helping a room seem larger?

5. Does the furniture in each room serve a purpose, creating space for people to gather?

Now, think of your home as if you are putting it on the market. Though you may have no plans to sell your home in the immediate future, learning to think along these lines will help raise your daily standards. Knowing the steps involved to prepare your home for a sale may propel you to make some needed home improvements. A fresh coat of paint can do wonders to brighten a room, as well as the mood of your home, and may be what inspires your family to better maintain your home.

Consider the strategy of the model home. A model home is set up to enhance the experience of each room. Shelves and cabinets are decorated but not crammed full. Colors are welcoming. Pathways are clear and floor space is optimal. The entrance is well lit. Cabinets are filled with just enough items for a family of four, or the number the home is designed for.

That same thought process applied to your home will dramatically change what is allowed inside. Real estate agents provide a checklist to those hoping to sell their homes; the list describes what must be done before the home is presentable to potential buyers. Once the to-do items on the list are complete, the house must maintain that state, always ready for a new visitor to scope it out.

The following is a checklist provided by real estate agent Tammy Spann of Keller Realty in Atlanta. Whether you have plans to place your home on the market in the near future, the following suggestions will help you view your home through a fresh perspective:

Realtor Guidelines for Preparing Your Home for Prospective Buyers

REALTOR GUIDELINES	
Room	**Notes for Improvement**
Outside the Home	Curb appeal matters most. Visitors spend a great deal of time looking at the front of the home. Prospective home buyers could decide at this point to drive away based on the outside appearance alone so determine what message the outside of your home sends.
	There should be no stains on the driveway.
	There should be no toys in the yard.
	The front porch area must be well lit; there should be no cobwebs; it should be swept clean; and there should be no chipped paint. Your guests will get a good feel for the house from the front porch alone.
	Remove all obvious sign of pets, such as food or water bowls, toys, and a leash or collar.
	The storm door and windows must be clean and free of fingerprints.
	Limit your external entrance to a simple welcome mat or door decoration.
	Include plants or flowers to add color to the entrance.
	Your yard must be well maintained and freshly mowed.
	Bushes and trees need to be trimmed and kept neat. Landscaping should never overpower the entrance to the home.
Inside the Home	Keep shades of paint to warm and neutral shades only; no startling colors.
	Clean all carpets and have them professionally stretched out if there are wrinkles in them from use over time. Remove any obvious carpet stains.
	Remove excess furniture to allow the room to speak for itself. Keep natural walkways completely open.
	Clean out closets. Any overcrowding in storage areas will translate into not enough storage space, regardless of how big the closets actually are.
	Use soft lighting to provide a natural welcome.
	Allow as much outside light in as possible by opening window shades or blinds.
	Empty all trash cans. No overflowing baskets allowed.

REALTOR GUIDELINES	
Room	Notes for Improvement
Kitchen	Wipe countertops free and clean of debris.
	Keep refrigerators free of pictures, paperwork, and magnets. This adds to the visual clutter of the kitchen.
	Ensure the cabinets and kitchen pantry remain uncluttered and organized.
	Drawers should be organized and roomy, filled with only items used in the kitchen.
	The kitchen area should be well lit and all workspaces kept open and free of knickknacks.
Bathrooms	Showers and bathtubs should be wiped clean.
	Decorative towels need to be hung neatly on racks.
	Excess clothing or robes should be removed from any over-the -door hangers.
	Place toilet seats and lids down.
Bedrooms	Beds should be neatly made.
	Keep walls plainly decorated. Too much is overwhelming.
	Put everything in its place.
	Keep closets easily accessible and the floor and shelves free of unnecessary items for that room.
Garage or Basement Area	Cabinets or storage areas should be easily accessible.
	Clean the floor free of any stains.
	Keep walls clear to emphasize the overall size of this area. If there are boxes or bins in this area, move them to the middle of the space so they will not diminish the size of the room.
	Store as many things up and out of reach rather than on the floor area.
	Neatly organize tools, sporting equipment, yard equipment, and bicycles.

What the experts consider as clutter

Your daily surroundings seem normal to your family, but may be considered cluttered to friends or visitors to the home. A real estate agent, professional decorator, or organizer can immediately identify what needs to be removed or changed as they enter a room, and you need to acquire this ability as well.

For example, bulletin boards covered in kindergarten art is beautiful to you but becomes junky and disorganized to the casual observer. A mail sorter by the front door with bills hanging out might serve as a reminder to you to make sure bills are paid on time but are unappealing to visitors. An overflowing toy box or trunk may be where the toys belong, but this might need to be scaled down or even removed in order to open up some space. Magnets, calendars, and photos that cover the refrigerator are special souvenirs of friends and family vacations but too much visual clutter becomes overwhelming to a new visitor to the home.

Room by Room Evaluation

As you walk through your home, notice the items that fall by the wayside and seem to have no home. With each item, ask yourself the following three questions:

1. When was the last time it was used?
2. Where is it used most often?
3. Would I take it with me if I were moving?

Answering these questions should help determine if the item is still needed, if it is worth keeping, and if so, where it should be stored. If that item goes unused for at least six months, remove it from your living space. If the desire for that item is no longer there, it signifies it is time to let it go. This works for anything: dishes, toys, books, furniture, clothing, backpacks, or handbags.

For toys, rotate them in and out, temporarily storing some in a plastic tub in an available closet for a predetermined time, possibly every three to four months, and then bring them back out at a later date. Rotating your child's toys in and out will keep the number of toys you have to manage at one time to a minimum, while teaching your children to appreciate and actually use the toys they have. With toys, sometimes absence makes the heart grow fonder. If your child loses interest over this time, it is time to get rid of that toy or pass it on to others.

You want your home arranged in such a way that your supplies and items are stored where they are used. Most school classrooms are set up using this method with special interest centers in each corner supplied with whatever is needed in that space. For example, the reading center has books, pillows, and comfortable chairs; the writing center provides paper, pencils, erasers, and notebooks; and the listening center has CD players, earphones, and shelves with books on CD. Your home will benefit from storing items where your family uses them.

Take the following checklist and go through your house room by room. Act as if you are seeing your home for the first time. As you go through each room, take note of what tends to gather there naturally. If your living room or family room always has an extra blanket or pillow left on the couch, those items need to be stored nearby. If backpacks and purses line the floor by the front door, establish a place to keep them. The problem areas of your home are likely already telling you what it needs more or less of so take notice.

Look up. Check the ceilings for cobwebs and signs of leaks. Make sure all windows are properly closed and that blinds or shades work properly. Allow for as much natural light as possible to improve the overall atmosphere in your home. Set a time to launder and iron all curtains, as well as dust your blinds. Wash windows, making sure to clean underneath them where dirt gathers through the screen. Change any burned out light bulbs, and remove all light fixtures and clean them. A well-lit home provides warmth and invites others. The same is true for outside your home.

"What to Watch For" checklist

Room	What to Watch For	Plan of Action
Entryway	Shoes and socks	Shoe stand with shelf
	Stacks of mail	Mail sorter for incoming or outgoing mail
	Coats or jackets	Use a coat rack
	Backpacks or handbags	Hooks or pegs on the wall
	Keys, cell phones, MP3 players, earphones	Hanging cubby box with pegs
	Forgotten items that stay too long	Every day, clear the area of anything that does not belong by the door
Living Room or Family Room	Make sure pieces of furniture do not obstruct the natural traffic flow	Keep your floor space free; never stack items on floor
	Books, magazines, videos, or papers left on tables or couch	Return everything to its proper location each evening
	Blankets and pillows left out on furniture	Stash these items in a nearby closet or ottoman
	Leftover signs of snack time: dishes, paper plates or cups, or wrappers	Only allow eating here if the kids clean up after themselves
Kitchen	Dishes left out	Put away if clean, in dishwasher if dirty
	Pens, pencils, and papers	Purchase a magnetic pad on refrigerator with one pen attached
	Stacks of mail on countertops	Process mail weekly
	Keys and cell phones left on counters	Set up cubbies in entryway

Room	What to Watch For	Plan of Action
Kitchen	Cabinets crammed with unused items	Store rarely used items neatly on top of cabinets
	Junk drawers overflowing with items not needed in the kitchen	Use organizers to only store what is needed in the kitchen; eliminate junk drawers
Laundry Room	Laundry and cleaning supplies	Store on shelves or in cabinets up high
	Wastebasket for lint from dryer	Wipe down washer and dryer weekly to control lint
	Special place to hang clothes needing to be dry cleaned or needing special attention	Designate a special hamper or hook for special-care clothing
	Sorter hanging baskets for dirty clothes	*Explained further in Chapter 5*
Bed-rooms	Books and papers on night-stands	Allow one book at a time by your bed
	Papers stacked on desk areas	Set up simple filing system
	Clothes or shoes on floor	*Explained further in Chapter 7*
	Leftover dishes, paper products, or wrappers from kitchen	Only allow this if your kids clean up afterward
	Any item not used in the bedroom	Determine a better home for that item
Bath-rooms	Trash area	Get basket large enough to hold trash for a week
	Counter tops, mirrors, sinks, and toilets	Clean weekly
	Drawers or cabinets	Only store what is used here
	Bathtub or shower area/shampoo bottles, razors, or soap	Store neatly in hanging basket
	Toothbrush holders or soap dishes	Soak in hot water with a cap full of bleach weekly
	Clothes hampers	Get hamper with handles to carry to laundry room
	Hanging area for robes, towels, etc.	Purchase over-the-door hooks

Room	What to Watch For	Plan of Action
Garage or Basement Area	Excess items stored in this area that interfere with the true purpose of this space	Use wall space and overhead shelves as much as possible to keep room for vehicles
	Similar items scattered in various places, such as sporting goods stowed in each corner	Buy caddy especially for sporting goods; hang bags on hooks on the wall
	Yard equipment out where children can access it	A corner caddy works well for garden equipment; store mowers and electric equipment, gasoline, and oil in a locked enclosure
	Tools disorganized and scattered	Lock tools and hardware in cabinets
	Riding toys, bicycles, and safety gear taking up all available floor space	Bicycle racks and hooks work well on the wall

Identifying danger zones

Danger zones are clean and empty spaces that quickly pull in new items to clutter them. The danger zones in your home usually reveal themselves within a couple hours after your home is cleaned. Table or countertops, desktops, entryways, empty chairs, and furniture quickly become the temporary home of unwelcome papers, jackets, mail, backpacks, and blankets or pillows. It requires diligent effort and easy solutions brought over time to conquer your danger zones.

Simple Entryway Solutions

The entryway to your home will command attention from you, even though it is not an actual room in the house. No matter how many times you clear this area, it will continue to become cluttered until you formulate a plan on how to deal with the things that gather here. For example, if you typically find numerous sets of keys waiting on the table by the front door, find a decorative key hanger and place it on the wall. If both incoming and outgoing mail are mixed in stacks on this same table, get a mail sorter and only use it for outgoing mail. That way, if anyone in the family needs something mailed, it goes in the slot and is mailed immediately without risk of it getting lost. *For tips on managing your incoming mail, see Chapter 13.*

Many families establish the practice of having everyone remove their shoes as they enter the home. This helps to preserve your carpet or flooring and eliminates a great deal of cleanup work later on. The problem with this practice is it keeps the front door area cluttered with shoes. If this is the case in your home, buy a shoe rack or stand so the shoes are placed or stacked rather than piled on the floor.

If you live in a colder climate where gloves, scarves, and hats are required, place an ottoman with storage, or a basket of some sort, in this area so all items are contained. This will help your family find matching gloves and ensure they cover their heads before heading out into the snow.

Also with colder climates comes the need for a coat rack and umbrella stand. This should mainly be used for visitors' coats and hats rather than for all the coats for your family. Your family's coats and hats should have a permanent storage place, such as the closet nearest to the front door. On rainy or snowy days, stretch a trash bag out so all wet items are spread out to dry as soon as people come through your door. Another option is to place an old towel beside your doormat to absorb the additional mud and moisture. Following these few tips should keep the dirt tracked in from the outside contained to your entryway rather than spread all over the house.

When looking to solve these problems, think vertical, and use your wall space. Here are some ways you can use the limited space in your entryway to properly manage your clutter:

- Hooks on the wall for coats or keys

- Coat racks with umbrella stands for guests

- Benches with storage underneath for purses or bags

- A shoe stand if shoes are removed inside the front door

- A mail sorter with slots for outgoing mail and cell phones

- A cubby system with assigned cubbies for each family member to hold their stuff as they come in the door

Here is an example of a shoe rack that can be used in entryways or closets.

Small Home Solutions

If your space is limited, you must also limit the amount of furniture and decorations you bring to that space. Keep in mind that less is more, and the space itself is your most valuable commodity. For smaller homes, first determine the minimum amount of supplies needed to live in your home. You most likely do not require dishes for 12 people or a large table that seats eight for your family of four. Your linen closet should not be overflowing with extra sheets, blankets, or towels that will not be used in your living space. If you do not have the space to accommodate company, it is not necessary to keep extra supplies on hand for visitors.

Europeans have been utilizing creative ways to live in small spaces in their crowded cities for hundreds of years so it would be wise to consider the ways they deal with the lack of space. IKEA even has a sample living space set up in their showroom, boasting a complete home that only requires 270 square feet of living space. This is made possible by using furniture that serves multiple purposes. Consider the following examples of furniture that enhances small spaces:

- Full-sized day bed with storage drawers underneath.

- Vanishing headboard shelves that are designed to face the wall. The front looks as if it is a solid headboard but behind are shelves that could store books and smaller items.

- A bedside table on wheels with an extended shelf that goes underneath the bed. When those items are needed, just swivel around for easy access.

- Stacking chairs or drop leaf tables that can be brought out as needed but stored when the open space is preferred.

- Hanging cabinets with doors. Shelving or cabinets on the wall draw your attention upward and make the room feel much more spacious.

- Decorative mirrors that add lighting and depth.

In America, the studio-size apartment is becoming more popular, especially in downtown cities. To furnish a studio apartment properly, plan to use all available space for a specific function, sometimes even serving several purposes at once. With limited space, you must take into consideration where something will be stored before ever bringing it into your home.

The Oprah Winfrey Show did an episode in 2006 that focused on creative pieces of furniture for small living spaces. If money is not a factor, consider the following:

- A desk that converts to a bed, without having to first clean off the desk. Off the Wall offers one at **www.offthewall-beds.com/bedsspecial.html**.

- An armless chair with a storage drawer underneath for keeping remotes and magazines. JCPenney offers one for $300.

- A coffee table where the top raises and forms a desk, revealing storage underneath, is available from Julia West Home.

- Off the Wall also offers a Library Bed. Bookshelves filled with books slide to the side, revealing a bed that folds down to the floor. Though it is costly at around $6,000, it is the ultimate space saver for the bedroom and provides elegance as well.

And, if money is a huge factor in your storage woes, you are not out of luck. Try some of these ideas:

- Get rid of the sofa and use several chairs instead. Arrange as needed, and open up your floor space for your friends.

- Hang curtains or place a room divider in a corner, creating hidden storage and adding decorations all at once.

- Use wall space for storage. Pans and utensils can be used as decorations, as can mirrors, jewelry, or a decorative blanket.

- Use the space between spaces. Buy a rolling cart 10 inches wide to store books and smaller items. You can use this in your bathroom, between furniture, and even the space between your refrigerator and cabinet.

- Buy a closet on wheels, available for $30. Hang canvas shelves inside and put a curtain across the front to take advantage of mobile storage solutions.

One of the most imaginative ways to create storage when space is limited is by using ottomans or benches that offer hidden storage. These work well in living rooms, family rooms, entryways, and even bedrooms. Many different vendors offer items with prices ranging from $40 to $400 so they can blend in easily with any décor. They are a great way to store extra pillows, blankets, and bed linens for guests. It is wise to fill them with items that will be used in the room they are in, such as magazines or extra blankets for the living room.

Uncluttering Family Areas

Regardless of the number of rooms your home has, your family is probably drawn to one or two areas. As much as everyone enjoys having their own space, they tend to gather in certain areas. It is time to focus on the areas where your family gathers to watch television, do homework, read, or invite friends over to watch a ballgame.

Your family room

Your family room should be an all-purpose room that serves the needs of everyone in the family without becoming overly cluttered with belongings. To keep the peace in your most-used room, try these suggestions:

- **Remote controls** — Stick a piece of fabric fastening tape on the back of each remote with another piece on the side of your television. If possible, program one universal remote so you do not have to press the buttons on four different remotes to determine which one controls which piece of equipment.

- **Video games** — House video games and game systems in a rolling cart with large drawers. Move this cart into the closet when the gaming system is not in use.

- **Small basket for baby and toddler toys** — Get a decorative basket with a lid to keep a few favorite toys in the family room. Toddlers are happy playing with almost anything, but they will enjoy having their own stuff in the room where everyone else spends most of their time.

Oppress the Mess

Tip #4

Leave Each Room in Good Condition

At the end of a night of family fun, such as watching a movie or playing games, leave the room in good condition. Ask one child to get the dishes and place them in the sink. Another family member can pick up the trash, and another can put away the games. Let them see that clean up always follows a fun event, and it can happen quickly with help.

Homework zones

Homework is a dreaded part of your children's lives. They find the idea of it stressful enough, so do what you can in order to set them up for success. These tips also work well for those families who decide to home school their children.

Here are a few suggestions for homework or home-schooling areas:

1. Store all school supplies in a designated location. Buy extras when they are on sale, normally prior to the first week of school. Having these items on hand will prevent a great amount of unnecessary stress later on for your children. Carefully organize the following on a shelf, in a desk, or in a plastic drawer set where they will remain out of sight:

Here is an example of an organized drawer of school supplies. The family uses a tray with plastic dividers to separate smaller items and plastic bags to keep rubber bands together. They also group together supplies and use rubber bands to keep writing utensils together.

   - Notebook paper
   - Pens and pencils
   - Erasers
   - Pocket folders
   - Three-ring binders with pockets
   - Section dividers
   - Glue
   - Scissors
   - Stapler with extra staples
   - Paper clips

2. To keep your children organized while they are at school, help them decide which supplies they need with them at

all times. As they get older and change classes or go from building to building, they may determine it is best to keep their backpack with them between classes throughout the day, so it needs to be stocked with pens, paper, pencils, and even a bottle of water and an occasional snack. Pack these items the night before school from the school supplies you keep in the home.

3. If at all possible, it is helpful to set a standard schedule for your home each evening. By serving dinner at the same time, your children will know how much time they have for homework before dinner, and they will look forward to the break. This should allow free time in your evenings, making it more enjoyable for everyone.

Craft areas

Being organized requires planning well in advance for what your family needs. There are times kids have special projects due for school that require even more supplies than what you may have in your home. Or, perhaps they pick up a hobby along the way that requires additional supplies. Either way, they need an area to do these tasks without taking over the kitchen table or other areas you hope to keep presentable. Think of this as setting up a special interest center. It may seem you are adding to the clutter of your home by doing this,

This family's playroom uses several systems to stay organized and uncluttered. The desk doubles as a craft area and the drawers below are used to keep craft supplies neat and categorized. The shelves and bins on the book shelf offer easy storage for toys. The cabinet drawers are used to store videos, board games, puzzles, video games, and cards.

but it will remove the frustration and panic that sets in when a school project is due. Being prepared for such moments will help.

Use your craft areas to create meaningful gifts for friends and family. But, because these items are used less frequently than your school supplies, you may wish to store them in a location that is not as readily accessible, such as in a rolling trunk in a spare bedroom or a closet. Consider some of the following items for your craft supplies:

- Poster board
- Tri-fold display boards
- Glue gun with glue sticks
- Clear sheet protector sleeves
- Spray paint in black or gold
- Markers
- Pipe cleaners
- Popsicle sticks
- Paint or watercolors
- Buttons
- String or thread
- Stickers
- Rubber bands

Determine where you should place this interest center. Buy a folding table used only for this purpose, and return it to storage when not in use. Many of these projects are long-term assignments that create a mess that must remain on the table for a week or so at a time. Before the school projects take over your home, decide where you will keep them.

Books and games

Playing board games together can be a great stay-at-home activity, even becoming a weekly tradition. Games are only fun to play when all the pieces are in place, and designing a workable, easily accessible place to store them will serve your family well. Jigsaw puzzles also work as a great group activity, allowing your family members to contribute for a few minutes at a time. Again, these activities should not take over the family dinner table. Determine a place to store these games and puzzles. Shelves work well, specifically the lower shelves where kids can have access to them. The same rule holds true for the books that belong to your family: Only keep what your family will use. As children grow and change so do their interest in books. They may no longer need their bedtime stories stored in their bedrooms as they begin reading longer books. When they begin required reading for school, keep the books you purchase for your older children, as your younger children will most likely need them later as well. As your family develops a collection of books, do not allow them to accumulate in your living areas. Keep them on shelves, or even in cabinets with doors, so they are not in full view.

Managing toys in your family areas

Because you have children, you also have an ample supply of toys. Without warning, your stash will multiply as your children bring home various stuffed animals, birthday party favors, and plastic toys from kids' meals at restaurants. Unless you outline a plan for them, the toys will soon take over all areas of your home.

Identify an easy-to-move toy box or a basket for babies and toddlers so you can take the box or basket to whichever room you are in, allowing your child to always have his or her toys nearby. When playtime is over, teach young children to return the toys back to the basket and put them out of sight. Also, keep in mind that kids of this age are content to play with anything, which can mean a group of measuring spoons, pots and pans, or a leftover shoe box. It is not necessary to purchase many toys, and your child will never know the difference.

As your children grow, their toys become bigger as well. Riding toys, such as tricycles and bikes, large stuffed animals, and dolls, are more difficult to store and keep hidden than the toys they used when they were babies. They may fill your family room on a daily basis, but return these toys to your children's bedrooms or playrooms each evening. This will reclaim the living area as one designed for everyone's enjoyment.

Pet areas

Depending on the size of your pet, it may be tricky to remove the evidence that it exists. For pets that remain in cages or crates, never allow their living quarters to be the main focus of the home. Aquariums with assorted colorful fish create a nice focal point in a room, but as a general rule, your goal should be to limit the signs that a pet lives in your home. Because dogs and cats quickly become part of the family, they may soon take over, but remember that your home belongs to you, and you are allowing the pets to live there. They must live in your home on your terms, following the rules you put in place. If not properly trained, a dog or cat can quickly ruin even the cleanest of homes. Pets are easiest to train when young, and much of their success comes when the pet owners are consistent. Limit their access to certain rooms of the house by closing the doors.

In caring for the home, if your pets shed on a regular basis, have them sleep in their own bed or area so your furniture and clothing are not covered with fur. Store your pet supplies, including snacks, toys, medicine, leashes, and collars, in a tub or crate out of sight. Keep a supply of plastic bags nearby for easy clean up of pet waste when you take your pet for a walk.

As for storing pet food, there are many creative options to consider:

- Purchase bagged pet food for one month at a time to keep it from getting stale.

- For large bags of food, consider a bin designed for holding charcoal. It is on wheels and has an easy-to-use flip top. Note they may only be available in stores during the summer months.

- Because some pets are known to tear into their bags of food, it may be necessary to store it in plastic cereal containers or pet food serving bins.

- Store dog or cat treats in glass canister jars with lids.

Realize the clutter pets bring with them is magnified with the addition of each pet. For this reason, you should keep the number of pets kept inside to a minimum. You must weigh the cost of the time and effort you spend trying to overcome the problem of pet hair, accidents, dirty paws, and pet odors to see if it is worth allowing them in the home. The addition of each pet hinders your chances of maintaining a neat and orderly home.

The next chapter addresses the very real impact that doing laundry has on your home. Laundry happens, and the amount of it multiplies with each family member. Ignoring it is not an option so outlining a plan of action will reign in this generally dreaded chore.

Chapter 5

Airing Your Dirty Laundry

In any home, it is impossible to gain control of clutter without dealing with the issue of laundry. For larger families, there may be as many as ten to 15 loads of laundry per week. As a parent, especially early on in the lives of your children, you will be the one doing the laundry. As you clean your family's clothing and linens each week, you have the best view of what needs to be repaired and what garments develop holes, stains, and other problems with clothing. If you notice certain items of clothing are no longer cycling through the laundry, it may be a sign to remove them so they do not take up valuable storage space in the closet.

Establishing your Laundry System

Before outlining how to do your laundry, you must first establish your own method of managing it. The following will happen if you do not have a plan of action for your family's laundry and it is left to its own accord:

- No one will be able to find what he or she needs when needed.

- Clothes that belong to one person will end up in the wrong room.

- Your kids will want to wear clothes in their hamper or lost somewhere in the laundry process.

- Your family members may leave the house wearing dirty or wrinkled clothes, something they may not notice until someone else brings it to their attention.

- The clean clothes brought to your kids' rooms will soon be combined with the pile of dirty clothes on the floor, causing them to be dirty by association.

Your laundry system will only work for your family if they know what to expect. If you plan to do laundry only on the weekends, all hampers should be brought to the laundry room on Fridays after school. As with any large task, it is better to break it down into portions rather than attempting to tackle the entire project at one time. With most large families, you need to do laundry several times a week so make sure your family knows the laundry schedule you intend on implementing.

Keep your children involved in the laundry process so they do not act as if some sort of Laundry Fairy comes into their room after they leave for school, picks up all their dirty clothes and towels, washes them, and magically returns them to their proper place before they get home from school. It is to your benefit and theirs if they understand how long it takes something to go through the washing and drying cycle. They should understand why a black pair of pants cannot be washed with a load of white clothes. Even if you do nothing more than pull up a chair and allow them to watch you put detergent in the washer while the water runs, they will learn to appreciate what is involved and will enjoy helping you.

Purchase a set of hanging sorting baskets, preferably the type with three separate baskets, so you can easily divide your laundry into three categories. Label each one with the way you want your laundry sorted in advance. Keep it simple, such as "Whites," "Dark Colors," and "Light Colors." Help your kids learn how to sort their own laundry. Even the youngest of children can follow this system, and it educates them early on as to how laundry is managed.

Providing each member of the family with his or her own laundry basket or hamper allows you to keep dirty clothes in a common spot and keep clothes separated.

Designate a particular location for clothes requiring extra attention, such as stains or something needed for a quick deadline. If your family understands a stain might come out if it is treated immediately or if their team uniform needs to be packed and ready by 8 a.m., they will invest some effort into making sure that item of clothing gets the attention needed to have it ready in time.

Color coding your family

A good way to simplify the process and generate some enthusiasm as you begin this new approach to managing your laundry is to assign a specific color to each family member. This color system works for hampers, laundry baskets, towels, hangers, and even socks or undergarments. Color coding removes the guesswork of trying to figure out which items of clothing belong to which member of your family. By doing this, you remove all doubt as to who brought his or her dirty laundry to the laundry room, and where it needs to go when it is complete.

For example, if your daughter likes the color pink, buy her a pink hamper, laundry basket, hangers, towels, and even socks with pink trim on them. After her clothes are washed, all her items will be returned to the pink laundry basket or placed on pink hangers. They can be purchased in bulk from The Container Store® at **www.containerstore.com** for less than $20 for a case of 72 hangers. If there are no pink towels in your sorted baskets of dirty clothes, chances are she is leaving them on the bathroom floor. She may soon find she is out of towels, so she will automatically be encouraged to put them where they belong. For socks, undergarments, and any other items that may be hard to decide who they belong to, use permanent marker in each family member's particular color to mark the item's tag. As you launch this system, it will give everyone a chance to go through the clothes in their closet, determining what is worth hanging up again on the new hangers.

Hampering hope — rules for clothes hampers

Hampers are available in various forms, from wicker to wood to a collapsible canvas hamper with wire side supports. Find hampers that blend in with the décor of each bedroom and that are easy to use. Because they will be used every day, place them where your family will use them every day, such as in bedroom or closet areas. Form rules for your hampers that include the following:

- Dirty clothes always go in the hamper, never on the floor.

- Wet clothes should never be placed in a hamper, or they will cause mold and mildew to other clothing. Hang them to dry before placing them in the hamper. This includes wet towels.

- Clean out pockets before placing clothes in the hamper. An entire load of clothes can be ruined by a leftover ink pen or tube of lip balm.

- Just because an item has been worn once does not mean it is dirty. Jeans, pants, dresses, or shirts can sometimes be worn a couple of times without becoming dirty. Place these items back in the closet or drawer to be worn again if they are clean.

Laundry Basics

Take a quick look at some tips on how to better perform the actual task of washing and drying your clothes; these are ideas to consider that may make this area of your life easier.

- Check all pockets in advance to remove notes, tissues, pens, crayons, or any other item that can wreak havoc during your washing cycle.

- Remove any nametags or stickers from clothing.

- Pretreat large stains with stain remover or laundry detergent. Once a stain is washed and dried, it is much more difficult to remove.

- Close any zippers, and fasten the clasps on bras to prevent snagging.

- Sort into whites, bright, and dark colors. Wash red clothes or other colors that might bleed separately.

- Separate towels, sweaters, and other items that produce lint from those items that attract it, such as fabrics like velvet, corduroy, and black pants.

- Place the correct amount of laundry detergent in your machine first and then turn on the water. Allow the detergent and water to work through the clothing before adding any fabric softener or bleach. Use automatic dispensers if your machine has them. If not, wait a few minutes and add during the wash or rinse cycle.

- Use hot water for whites.

- Cold water prevents fading of vivid colors and shrinkage. Use the cold rinse cycle for all clothing to conserve energy.

- Start the washer, and allow it to fill with water before adding clothes. This allows the detergent to dissolve completely into the water. If using bleach, pour that in as well so it can be equally dispersed. Do not overfill with clothes, as they need plenty of room to move around in order to become as clean as possible.

- Clear the lint trap from the dryer between each load. To remove buildup from fabric softening sheets on the lint trap, wash once monthly with dishwashing liquid, scrubbing the mesh until water flows freely through it. Allow it to dry completely before returning it to your dryer. By cleaning your lint trap on a regular basis, you will add to the life of your dryer and also prevent a possible fire from lint buildup that grows too hot.

- Most shrinkage occurs in the dryer so use medium heat as often as possible. Though it takes a little longer, it is easier on your clothes, as well as your dryer.

- Hang delicates to air dry.

- Lay sweaters flat to dry to prevent shrinkage or stretching. You can hang them when they are damp but not drenched.

- Once a month, run the empty washing machine using the hot water cycle and 2 cups of vinegar. This will remove any foul odors and will keep the parts clean as well. Wipe down the inside when this cycle is complete. Also, clean lint traps for the washer at this time.

- For those delicate items that require hand washing, use the water temperature recommended on the label. Fill a sink with water; add a few drops of laundry detergent, liquid dish soap, or even shampoo; and allow the clothes to soak. Rub the fabric together to remove any particularly dirty spots, and rinse until the water runs clear. Wrap in a towel to squeeze the excess water from your clothes, and then either hang to dry or place on a low cycle in your dryer.

Correcting laundry mishaps

There are those occasions when mistakes happen, sometimes affecting an entire load of clothing. Try these options to repair the damage:

- If an entire load of laundry is wrinkled after being left in the dryer for an extended time, run it through a ten-minute cycle with a damp towel.

- Use baby oil and a scrub brush on the residue left on clothing from a sticker or nametag.

- Sour-smelling clothes, caused by either leaving wet clothes in the washer too long or by clothes remaining damp in the dryer after the cycle completes, can be easily fixed. Fill the washer with water, detergent, and 1 cup of baking soda. Place sour-smelling clothes in the water only after the water has reached the top, and only place half a load of clothing in so all items can move about freely. During the rinse cycle, add 1 cup of white vinegar. This will also help to remove any remaining musty smell from within your washer.

- If an ink pen somehow sneaks into your washing machine, it is best to treat it while it is still wet. Place the item on a towel, and blot the stain with rubbing alcohol. The stain will begin to bleed onto the towel underneath so continue moving your clothing to a fresh spot on the towel. If any stain still exists after using alcohol, repeat the procedure using non-acetone nail polish remover. Then, re-wash any affected articles of clothing.

- For a load of white clothes that comes out of the washer tinted pink or blue, try to repair the damage before placing them in the dryer. First, remove the offending blue or red item that caused the problem. Second, get some RIT Color Remover® for whites from your laundry supply aisle, and soak these clothes. You can also run them back through the wash cycle using hot water and a cup of bleach, allowing them to soak for a while.

- If a sweater comes out of your dryer in a much smaller size than when you started, try soaking it in a bucket of water with a capful of hair conditioner. Lay flat on a towel to dry, stretching it frequently throughout the drying process.

Tips for hard-to-wash items

With a family of any size and age, consider the following tips for those articles of clothing that are difficult to wash in the typical way.

- **Baseball caps** — Pretreat stained areas, particularly in the band that fits around the head where sweat builds up. Wash in the top rack of the dishwasher, either attaching it with clothes pins to the rack or by placing it in a baseball cap shaper that helps to maintain its shape. This device can also work in the washing machine, or you can wash with shampoo in the shower. Always hang it to dry, leaving it in the shaper or placing over a large coffee can or bowl to retain its shape.

- **Tennis shoes** — For canvas tennis shoes, pretreat any stains, scrubbing with a toothbrush. Remove laces and wash in the washer with detergent and baking soda to eliminate odors from the shoes. Consider washing alone. Set out to dry. For leather shoes, especially those that are white, use a bathroom cleaner, such as Dow Scrubbing Bubbles® or a Mr. Clean® Magic Eraser®. Scrub and wipe clean.

- **Backpacks or duffle bags** — Wash alone in the washing machine, making sure to remove all articles from pockets in advance. Use baking soda with detergent to eliminate any odors. If the backpack contains any foam or rubber lining, hang to dry. If not, it should be fine for the dryer.

- **Comforters** — Most comforters are too large to wash in a home washing machine. If the tag recommends it, take to a dry cleaner at least twice a year. If not, find a front-loading, industrial-size machine at a laundromat and wash there. Use cooler water and mild, liquid detergent that has a degreaser. Dry on low heat, throwing a clean tennis ball in with the comforter to keep it fluffy as it dries. Or if you prefer, hang it to dry. For a quick refresher between washes, toss in the dryer at home, if it fits, for ten minutes on low heat with an anti-static dryer sheet. If not, hang it outside in the sun on a breezy day, and let nature take care of it.

- **Pillows** — Get pillow protectors for your bed pillows that can be washed frequently, as bed pillows do not typically hold up well in the washer. Check all tags to see which of the pillows in your home are machine washable. For sofa pillows, remove the zippered covers and consider the care instructions for both the pillow and the cover. For those that work well in the washer, wash on the delicate cycle. Dry on low heat, adding a tennis ball to keep it moving and retain as much fluff as possible. For an in-between re-fresher, toss pillows and covers in the dryer with a tennis ball for a few minutes with a dryer sheet. This removes dust mites and fluffs them up.

- **Shin guards or knee pads** — These can be placed in the washing machine. Allow them to air dry before placing them back where they belong.

Time savers

The act of doing laundry should not take over your life, but it is a big part of daily survival. Here are a few suggestions to help incorporate laundry duties into your daily routine so you keep it under control:

- Remove clothes immediately from the dryer to prevent wrinkling.

- Have your kids bring their empty hangers (color coded) to the laundry room when clothes are being washed. Keep hangers close by, and hang all clothing that needs it.

- Start a load of laundry only when you will be nearby to move the clothes from the washer to the dryer.

- You may want a fourth laundry basket for "Special Instructions." This would include sweaters that need to be hung dry or permanent press items. Any items that need to be scrubbed in advance or have a recent stain can go here as well.

- Set a schedule for laundry, either every other day or twice a week. When everyone in your home knows what to expect, they are more likely to cooperate.

- Rotate turns for your kids to pick up any hanging towels in the bathrooms and allow them to wash a load of towels — including drying, folding, and returning to their proper places. These are the easiest to wash, only take a few minutes to fold, and will teach your kids to think of everyone's laundry, not just their own.

- Require everyone to use their same towel repeatedly, especially girls who tend to use one towel for their hair and another for their body. Make sure there is a place in each bathroom for towels to hang dry. This will cut down on laundry and conserve energy.

- If you separate clothes into color-coded baskets for each family member, take those into the family room while your family watches TV, and use that time for folding. Everyone can fold his or her own clothes without having to pay much attention to it. Use a rolling cart with extra hangers so the items that require hanging are placed immediately on hangers. When the TV show is over, have your family members take all their clothes to their room and put them away immediately. They can be finished within ten minutes, and you will be thankful to not have several baskets of clean clothes waiting for you after a long day.

• If you have a great amount of ironing, do it all at once so you are not rushing through it before you have to head to work or take the kids to school. Listen to some music, or iron while your clothes are washing. The time will pass quickly, and you will be thankful to have your clothes already wrinkle-free in advance of when you plan on wearing them, avoiding a last-minute ironing job when it is time to run out the door.

Sock it to 'em — winning the battle over socks

Socks seem to have a mind of their own at times, and they magically disappear just by going through the weekly cycle of laundry. They become mismatched, which leaves them unused and taking up space.

If you can first develop a way to know which socks belong to which family member, you will be well on your way to winning your battle over socks. Use a permanent marker to mark them with initials, or color code them as mentioned previously. When washing them, place a large rubber band that is strong enough to hold through both the washer and dryer cycles around each pair. Or, you may prefer a color-coded bag just for socks and undergarments, sometimes referred to as a lingerie bag. Using this type of bag allows socks to remain together throughout the washer and dryer cycle, eliminating wasted time spent searching later.

As you work through the laundry, throw away socks that have holes in them. Throw them away in pairs so an unmatched sock does not cause you to waste time searching for a mate that no longer exists. Plan to replace socks each year, perhaps before the start of a new school year, and get rid of all the old ones; your child should have no need for 20 pairs of socks at one time.

Just in case you want to keep a few of your mismatched socks, here are suggestions on how to use them creatively:

- Create a reusable, hot compress by placing uncooked long rice (not instant) in a long, athletic-type sock, and tie the end. Warm in the microwave for two minutes to use as a heating compress around your neck or feet. Add a drop or two of scented oil like eucalyptus or mint for a relaxing aroma.

- This idea also works as a cold compress if you freeze the rice bag for 45 minutes. Repeat this process as needed if you need to cool the rice again.

- Use old socks over your hands for cleaning and dusting.

- Use sheets to clean dirt and lint off your tile and wood floors.

- Cover shoes with them when packing for trips, making sure no dirt from the shoes gets on the surrounding clothes.

- Store larger shampoo, body wash, or lotion bottles in the socks when packing for trips in case there is a leak along the way. The sock will absorb most of the gooey mess and protect your other items when in transit. Store the sock-covered bottles in a gallon-size plastic bag to further protect your surrounding items.

De-Wrinkling Your Time — How to Prevent Wrinkles

Most children do not seem to notice if they leave the house with wrinkled clothes; however, most mothers or fathers do. Though you as a parent may be more embarrassed than your children if they leave in wrinkled clothing, you always want them to look their best and feel presentable. Because they are normally getting ready in a hurry and rushing out the door, sometimes without taking a look in a mirror, you may need to look for wrinkled clothing on their behalf. Some newer dryers are designed with steam features that diminish this problem as much as possible. But, here are some additional things you can do to prevent wrinkles from happening:

- Hang as many of your clothes as possible. If space allows, you should even hang your children's T-shirts. Lighter weight clothes wrinkle the easiest.

- For those clothes stored in your dresser drawers, try rolling them and placing them side by side instead of stacking them on top of each other.

- Look for fabrics that are wrinkle-free. Many fabrics are pretreated with anti-wrinkle finishing agents before being assembled. Lycra is being added to denim and cotton, allowing it to stretch and minimize wrinkles.

- If you notice wrinkles forming and have plans to wear a particular item of clothing, hang it in the bathroom before you take a shower. The steam will help the wrinkles disappear.

- Purchase a de-wrinkle spray, and use on an article of clothing before you plan to wear it. Run your hand over the clothing to smooth the wrinkles while it is still wet.

- Purchase a portable steamer. Run this quickly over your clothing without having to iron it completely.

CASE STUDY: MICHELLE MORTON, FORMER PROFESSIONAL ORGANIZER

Michelle Morton
Raleigh, NC
michellermorton@gmail.com

Michelle Morton is a former professional organizer who elected not to keep her company when her family relocated to Raleigh. A mother to three very active boys ages 14, 11, and 7, she continues to use her organizational skills to instruct her sons and manage her own household. Her family lives quite simply, keeping their belongings to a minimum and their home easy to maintain. She regards closets as her specialty, recognizing that if she cannot find it or maintain it, her boys will not make the effort to do so either.

Morton makes a practice of going through her boys' clothes at the change of every season to get rid of unused items. She donates whatever possible and occasionally sells through consignment, reusing that money to buy new clothes for her kids because they grow out of them so quickly.

She recommends that parents establish a morning and evening routine so everyone knows what to expect. By doing one small job at a time, it prevents your tasks from stacking up. For larger families where several people must share space, she encourages them to divide the space so each person is responsible for their own stuff in their own area.

Keeping kids involved in the process is the key to making your system work for your family.

"It is important to de-clutter before you try to reorganize," Morton said. "Don't buy a bunch of storage bins to simply hide things away. Get rid of your excess stuff first; then, figure out where to put what is left. Always keep it to a minimum."

One of Morton's favorite tricks are to reuse food containers, such as butter or ice cream containers with lids, to store prepackaged or loose snack foods on her pantry shelf. She is in the process of starting her own blog, which will also include a video feature, spotlighting the humorous side of her life as a mom to three boys, and will be entitled "Meet Michelle."

One of the most important things you can do for your family is to lead by example by using what is in your closet. If you have a closet full of clothes your family never sees you wear, they will follow suit. Make sure your closet is only filled with items you wear on a regular basis.

Oppress the Mess

Tip #5

Spot on. Spot off.

Spot clean items in your home as soon as a spill takes place. Whether it is on carpet, furniture, or clothing, your best chance to remove the stain comes from treating it immediately. Laundry sticks work great for clothing. Spray-on cleaner and a brush can dramatically improve the look of upholstered items or carpet, as long as it is done right after the spill takes place. Allowing it time to set in invites the stain to become permanent.

The quest to unclutter starts with reorganizing the closets in your home. Whether you have ample closet space or very little, you will learn to maximize your space and display only the items you use. It is time to reclaim and redefine your closets.

Chapter 6

Claustrophobic Closets

When fighting the ongoing battle of clutter in your home, consider your closets a close ally to help you achieve your goals. By taking control of your closet space, you are one step closer to permanently taking control of the home environment. Though no one ever claims to have too much closet space, the truth is that the amount of stuff you own grows until you fill the space that you have. Closet space is valuable so carefully evaluate each item in your closet and realize it must earn the right to be stored there. Each closet should be well organized rather than being used as a quick way to stash things out of sight that do not have a designated home.

To assist with this task, go on a treasure hunt in your home to identify hidden and overlooked spaces in and around your bedrooms that also work well for storage. Rediscovered storage space is an added bonus for a home that is taking a stand against clutter.

Hidden Treasures

In order to free up as much closet space as possible, take note of the valuable space you do not currently use. Take a look over, under, up, and down. Scan your wall and door space, and keep the floor clear as much as possible.

Over-the-door storage

Closet or bathroom doors that are not bi-fold or sliding doors offer a great source for available storage. Over-the-door racks and hooks are readily available at any department store. They vary in size, and some even include a shelf or an additional hanging bar that allows you to hang clothes on hangers. They are also available for pantry doors. This variety includes several shelves if you need shelving for smaller items, such as canned goods, but in your closet, these items can be used for everything from books to DVDs.

The back of the bedroom or closet door also serves as a good spot for a wall mirror. This will help keep clutter from building behind your doors because your children will need this space to check their appearance on a daily basis.

Under the bed

In an effort to keep items used on a regular basis nearby, you should take the inconspicuous but important space under the bed into consideration. Products are now designed specifically for space under the bed to store and organize everything from gift wrap (complete with tape, scissors, and tags) to shoes and books. Garment bags and wide, flat plastic drawers now have wheels so they can be pulled out easily when needed. This space may provide just the solution for your storage of seasonal clothing, as it allows you to keep these items in a safer environment than the basement or attic offer, while still freeing up valuable closet space.

Up the wall

When you need to create more space, remember to think vertically. Using your wall space as close to the ceiling as possible stretches the look of your room or closet. Taller shelves provide more storage without subtracting floor space.

Add hooks, pegs, or tie racks along the wall of your closet to hang hats, jackets, purses, belts, or backpacks. Add as much additional shelving as possible, making sure to use every corner of your closet space. Stackable cubes, also known as modular cube storage, work well in closets, providing versatility and convenience. These come in plastic or wood finish, and vary in size to fit your needs. If you have a tall wall space to fill, stack four of them, or stack a row of two at the bottom of your closet. The cubes have an open front and can be used as shelves, or you can slide canvas baskets or drawers into them.

Down below

As a general rule, you should keep the floor space in your closet, as well as throughout your home, as free as possible. Keep shoes organized in boxes or on a rack rather than cluttering the floor in a mismatched pile. You can choose to install more shelves, or add stackable shelves if necessary. Use the corners of the closet. Keep any clothing that hangs to the floor on one end of your closet, out of the way.

Be aware of the space you have underneath your hanging clothes. Most hanging clothes only take up about 3 feet in length of wall space so if the area below is available, use it to your advantage. If there is room to put in a small cabinet, dresser, or stacking plastic drawers, this may help free space in other areas of your bedrooms. Keep it organized, and stick to your rule of only storing what is used on a regular basis in that area.

The Secret Weapon

By maximizing the space in your closet, no matter how limited it is, and designating a home for every item, your closet becomes more of a weapon than a hindrance. Once closets are functional and organized and are used to store only the items used in that room, they will restore order to your bedroom areas.

Though it may be difficult to do, imagine each of your closets as if all the doors were removed. The trend in dorm rooms or other small spaces is to remove closet doors that get in the way and hang curtains over the closet's doorframe. For those with closets attached to a private master bathroom, sometimes the doors are removed to create a larger dressing area. If your closets were highly visible storage space, how would you organize it to be most useful and to keep it looking its best? If you were to remove the doors of your children's closets, would they be more likely to pay attention to how it looks and better maintain that space?

Removing the doors makes both the room and the closet seem much larger, and the fact that all your items are visible inspires your family to keep their closets straight. If you decide to do this, install as much shelving as possible, buy bins or baskets for each shelf, and add curtains to the doorway, tying them back in the middle as if they covered a window.

Sticky Note Game

A good way to get the family involved and to determine what is currently stored in your closets is to make a game of it. Give everyone in your family some sticky notes, possibly even in their assigned colors, so you can recognize which note belongs to which member of your family. Have them go to their closet and write on the notes what is stored in their closet. Then, have them do the same thing to coat closets or other family storage areas, writing one category or word on each note.

In your bedrooms, your notes may read as follows:

- Shoes
- Dress shirts
- Dresses/skirts
- Pants/jeans
- Backpack
- Luggage
- Toy box
- Purses

For your linen closet, your notes may read like this:

- Sheets and pillowcases
- Blankets
- Towels and washrags
- Extra toilet tissue

The categories written on these notes will help identify what does and does not belong. If sporting equipment or doll collections are taking over your children's closet space, this is keeping them from using those closets as they are intended to be used. If your linen closet is full of games and videotapes, it is thwarting the purpose for that closet — and more importantly, hindering your chances in the quest to overcome clutter.

Take a look at your notes and first pay attention to what does not fit; items like pet toys, old costumes, or photo albums do not belong in a linen or bedroom closet. Let your children remove the notes listing items that do not fit the purpose of that space, and then remove those corresponding items as well. Everything stored in your closet must earn the right to be there. There is no room for clothes that no longer fit, that are out of season, or that are no longer worn.

After your family places notes on all the closets in your home, ask them to rearrange the notes in such a way that makes more sense, remembering to keep similar items together. Feel free to use this note game to categorize drawer space as well. By categorizing your items as you reorganize your home, your children will soon understand why something belongs in a certain drawer, spot, or in the closet rather than just stuffing their clothes anywhere. For younger children, you can use pictures. They can recognize where shoes and socks should go. Let them put a picture on each drawer of where they think their pants, shorts, shirts, or under-wear should be kept. Though they may need your guidance, they will begin to understand the process of organizing their space. Making a game out of this may take much longer than just doing it yourself, but your children will learn to manage themselves along the way. Children learn by solving problems so always make them a part of your solutions.

The Dreaded Bedroom Closets

Many people hold onto items they no longer need or use because they offer great sentimental value. As a general rule, people have trouble parting with old prom dresses, children's first outfits, or any other article of clothing that has special memories. You may even hold onto a favorite outfit, hoping to fit into it again one day or relishing the thought of how you once looked in that color or style.

Be aware of these emotional ties as you sort through your belongings. If you view each of your belongings from a practical standpoint rather than an emotional or sentimental standpoint, it will be easier to determine what goes and what stays. One way to think through this is to envision how you would explain your system to someone else. Does it make sense when you say it out loud? If someone asks what percentage of the clothes in your closet you wear on a regular basis, how would you answer? For those clothes you keep just in case they are needed, or because of great memories they bring, this is an emotional attachment rather than a practical one. If your clothes no longer serve their practical purpose, it is time to discard them.

Cleaning out the closets

Save an entire day for cleaning out the bedroom closet. Allow yourself plenty of room to spread the items out so you can try them on as you go. Get five tubs with lids and label each one into one of the following categories:

- Keep it — keep only items that fit and are used on a regular basis.

- Donate it — give away items that would serve someone well but are no longer used.

- Sell it — plan to sell fully functional items your family outgrew.

- Mend it — only hold onto items that are easily repaired and are guaranteed to be worn again after repair.

- Trash it — throw away items that are damaged beyond repair, undergarments, or socks.

You may wish to get a sixth tub or basket used simply for items that need to be returned to another location. Having this sixth basket will keep you from running from room to room as you go along, prolonging an already difficult job.

This is not an easy process, and it takes time to do correctly. Pick up each item of clothing. Take time to try it on, making sure you can move freely in each outfit and that it still fits you properly. Remind yourself why you liked or disliked wearing that item. Look in a full-length mirror, and take note. If you have not worn that item in a long time, determine what the reason is.

- Was the fabric itchy or uncomfortable?

- Did it wrinkle too much throughout the day?

- Is the hem of the pants too long, causing it to stick on the heels of your shoes?

- Does a button frequently pop open?

- Is it too tight or loose?

- Does the color or style look wrong on you?

- Does the outfit lower your self-confidence for some reason?

This is your day to make the decision about each article of clothing. Plan to only touch an article of clothing once, deciding right then where it is going next. Either it is leaving your home, going to a temporary form of storage for your seasonal belongings, or returning to your closet. Be honest with yourself so you can carefully measure the chances of whether you ever plan on wearing that piece of clothing again. Keeping an item until you decide what to do with it is not an option, nor is keeping it until you lose weight. A closet full of clothes that no longer fit sends a daily negative message to you. Reward yourself with new clothing once you meet your weight goals, if this is the reason why you are holding onto so many items of unworn clothing.

Do not stop until the job is finished. Immediately remove the clothes you are donating or throwing away. If you do not have the means to sell the nicer items at a consignment or garage sale in the near future, donate all of your unused clothing. It is not worth your time, energy, or space to hold onto items for a long time, hoping to later sell them. If you do not like an item of clothing, you will not wear it so give yourself permission to discard it. Once you decide to donate an item of clothing, refer to Chapters 12 and 13 on options for charity donations and how to sell your items.

Professional hanging systems

The increasing number of companies that offer custom closet organization is a sign of our cluttered times. Each of these companies install as many shelves and hanging bars as possible to maximize the available wall space within your closet area. There are many types of storage systems available, ranging from inexpensive wire systems at your local department store to custom-built wood systems worth thousands of dollars. Borrow ideas from magazines and professional closet system websites, such as Easy Closets at **www.easyclosets.com**, or Closet and Storage Concepts® at **www.closetandstorageconcepts.com/closet.htm**.

Regardless of how much money you have available to spend on this project, you must maximize your space to the fullest. Measure the space you have available, and consider how to best use it. If you do not wish to install and attach a complete hanging system to the walls in your closet, purchase stacking shelves or modular

Here is an example of a custom closet hanging system. Because the closet is narrow, the homeowners included multiple shelves to keep the floors clear of clutter.

cubes that are user-friendly for small children. Keep them low where the kids are more likely to use them. Some varieties even come with attachable doors, creating mini-lockers so your children can compartmentalize their belongings.

Temporary hang-ups

If you are not able to permanently install a new organizational system for each closet, consider these available options. Though less sturdy, they are less expensive and still provide additional storage space where none existed before.

- **Buy plastic hangers in various colors.** As discussed in Chapter 5, purchase lightweight hangers in bulk, which are available in many colors at discount stores. The plastic hangers also space the clothing nicely, making it easier for little hands to manage, and clothing becomes tangled less frequently.

- **Buy space-saving hangers.** Use some of the new, tiered space-saver hangers for pants and skirts. These hangers cascade downward, instantly creating more space by hanging five to ten garments in a space that previous only allowed room for one garment. These hangers are available at any department store, some with clips specifically for skirts or pants.

- **Buy a tie/belt rack for each closet.** These come in various styles, are inexpensive, and work well for many items besides ties, including belts, scarves, leotards, and lingerie. Determine which of the following styles work best for your needs in each particular closet.

   1. A tie rack built like a clothes hanger to hang over your closet rod. .

   2. A "twirl a tie" rack that hangs over your closet rod but is an extended circular device with individual pegs. It is easier to retrieve your items when needed from this style.

   3. A wall-mounted tie rack with individual pegs.

   4. A motorized tie rack that revolves to display your choices with the push of a button.

   5. A free-standing tie rack that sits atop a dresser or deep shelf.

- **Hanging canvas shelves.** These are reinforced with heavy cardboard and designed for lightweight items. They come in all sizes, and provide storage solutions for shoes, purses, sweaters, jeans, and even team uniforms. Some companies even offer a six-shelf daily organizer for kids labeled with the days of the week, combining the weekend days onto one shelf, which is perfect for younger children to store everything they need to get ready for school each day.

- **Over-the-door pocket organizer.** This serves as a great catch-all for smaller items, such as socks or hosiery, hair clips, clutch bags, wallets, jewelry, or undergarments.

- **Spring-mounted shower curtain rod.** If you are still short on space and permanent solutions, use a wide expandable shower curtain rod to create another hanging bar near the top of your closet. Make sure it is secured, and do not hang heavier items on this, but it can work as a temporary solution for hanging lightweight blouses or skirts.

Tip #6

O p p r e s s t h e M e s s

Must-have items for every child's closet.

- **Hanging shelf system.** These allow kids to manage their week at a glance. Their uniform for the game on Saturday can be stored on one shelf, and you can fold school uniform shirts and store on each shelf to represent each day of the week. Add socks and undergarments, and they will know what to expect in advance without wondering if their clothes are clean and ready to go.

- **An over-the-door organizer,** with plenty of pockets for the smaller items, such as doll or car collections.

- **A fun hamper.** You can find collapsible hampers that take the form of anything from hungry bears to frogs to fire hydrants or basketball nets. Keep the hamper on ground level, low enough for your children to reach. You can find many unique hampers from Hayneedle at **http://closet organizersource.com**.

- **A shoe rack.** These provide a low and easily accessible location for shoes. Make sure to remove shoes that your child has outgrown or are out of season. If there is a chance your child can wear shoes the following season, store them with his or her other seasonal items.

Restoring Order

The best tip to organizing a closet is to start from scratch. By removing everything from your closet at once, you are free to reclaim your space and make it work for you. Consider the organizational tactics of department stores. They display it by keeping similar items together, usually in colors from lightest to darkest. Matching accessories, such as scarves, jewelry, and belts, are nearby and easily accessible. Displaying your clothing by category and color keeps them looking neat, makes clothes easy to find, and is the best way to maintain your new system in the future. Here are some guidelines you can implement to keep your closet clean and organized:

- While your closet is empty, vacuum it out completely. Wipe down the shelves and spray some air freshener.

- Group clothing by category, placing skirts together, pants together, dresses together, and shirts together.

- Group suits at one end of the closet, away from frequent handling to protect them.

- You may wish to organize your closet according to where clothes are worn. You can place work and special occasion clothing in one area and casual clothing in another.

- Separate short sleeved shirts and blouses from long sleeved items.

- Group by color, from lightest to darkest, in each area.

- Take any items that need repair to a seamstress. Do not store them in your closet until they are ready to be worn.

This will prevent you from leaving in a hurry in an outfit that is missing a button or has a broken zipper.

- Place a small trash can in your closet, or hang a trash bag on a hook. Use this trash can to dispose of debris from pockets, tags from new clothing, or loose threads from clothing.

- Have a plan for special care items. Either use a garment bag to protect them, or designate a special location in the closet to store them until they are properly cleaned.

- Remove any items that no longer fit properly or have permanent stains. You may wish to keep a bag on a hook in your closet strictly to store items you wish to donate as you decide to discard them.

- Keep a small stepstool in your closet to reach items stored above where you can easily reach.

- Mount hooks in your children's closets for backpacks or jackets. As they grow older, you can add a row of hooks above these.

- Use a baseball cap rack or wall hook to hang caps so they can air out after use. Make sure these are placed with team uniforms before game time. Baseball cap racks come as decorative wooden shelves if you wish to make it a part of your children's wall décor, or install a wire or plastic rack inside a closet. *For additional tips on cleaning baseball caps, refer to Chapter 5.*

Once you have your clothing in place, make a point to keep all empty hangers in one area. For example, if you have two clothing rods in your closet, move all empty hangers to the bottom rod as clothing is removed from them. This will keep the empty hangers from becoming tied up with other clothing and will always provide a ready supply. As freshly laundered clothes come out of the dryer, these hangers are readily available so the clothes can quickly be returned to the closet. This eliminates wrinkles and keeps the room from being re-cluttered by a newly arriving basket of clean clothes.

Handling handbags, purses, backpacks, and totes

Many factors determine how many handbags or purses a woman owns. Women with young children tend to use a diaper bag to carry their personal belongings, as well as items their children need. Some women carry a larger, all-purpose bag, while others change bags frequently to match their shoes or attire. Regardless of your preference, you need a way to manage the bags that find their way into your closets. Here are a few suggestions for storing them:

- Hang a plastic toy storage chain with hooks in the corner of your closet. These are designed for stuffed animals or small toys, and extra hooks can be purchased as needed. Hook handbag or tote handles to each clip. This may not work for nice, leather purses or those with decorative straps.

- Organize purses in a row on a shelf, almost like a row of books.

- Look for a hanging handbag pocket file. These offer clear, vinyl pockets for each handbag, and protect them from dust while preserving the purse straps.

- Install an expanding hook rack or individual hooks on the back side of your closet door or closet wall.

- Place them in stacking modular cubes or on shelves lining the wall.

Shoe fly shoo

One last item to conquer in your closet is shoes. Shoes tend to scatter to the corners of your home so start by gathering all your shoes in your room with the intention of downsizing your collection.

- Throw away any shoes with holes in the bottom, broken heels, or with ripped soles.

- Determine if any shoes are worth repairing, and take them to a repair shop. Sometimes a good polishing and heel reinforcement can add to the life of your shoes, especially men's shoes.

- Discard or donate any that are so uncomfortable you avoid wearing them at all cost.

- Do you have any duplicates, such as three pairs of black pumps, or four pairs of white tennis shoes? If so, choose the pair in the best condition, or the ones that are most comfortable, and keep that pair. Discard any others.

- Store those shoes that are in season and worn regularly on a shoe rack. You can use a horizontal rack, which is stored on the floor of your closet, or a vertical rack, which is narrow and works well in the corners or against the wall. Hanging shoe racks that are designed for the back of the closet door work well if you have a walk-in closet with non-folding doors.

- For out-of-season shoes that are in good condition and that will be worn again, store them in clear, plastic containers on shelves at the top of your closet or with other out-of-season apparel.

- You may wish to attach your boots with a rubber band or tie them so they stay together. Slide the cardboard rolls from wrapping paper inside so they will not fall over. Place them in a hanging cubby or cube, or keep them in their original box on a shelf. If you have several pairs, take a picture of each one to attach to the outside of the box so you can keep them straight.

Storage for Seasonal Items

While you organize your closets, you should only use space for items you are currently using. If closet or drawer space is already overcrowded, your family is less likely to take the time to return items to their proper location because people are more likely to leave items out when they do not know what to do with them. For example, no one should be filtering through heavy coats in the middle of August in order to find a favorite summer dress or put their shorts away.

Make sure you only store items you know you will use again the next season, particularly if your children are still growing. Though it is difficult to predict when your children will experience growth spurts, it is wise to use the change of seasons to get rid of clothing that no longer fits. As you place your seasonal items in storage containers, only store clothing that still offers your children growing room.

Creative seasonal storage options

Here are a few more creative options for storing seasonal items:

- Vacuum-sealed space saving bags. These are fairly new to the market and work well for clothing, pillows, and blankets because the bags keep these items as compact as possible. Space Bag®, available at **www.spacebag.com**, offers a product that is airtight and waterproof. The largest versions can store the equivalent of three king-sized comforters and four pillows, shrinking them into an easy-to-manage, stackable bag no more than 12 inches high. These hold up to four times more than plastic bins can store, and they are easily reusable. Though wrinkling may be more of an issue using this method, you may prefer knowing your seasonal items are under your bed nearby and well protected from the elements and critters that come with storing these items in the basement or attic. Ziploc® offers extra large bags in 3, 5, 10, and 20 gallon sizes. These are called Ziploc Big Bags and are sturdy and store easily.

- Wicker trunks are great for clothing because they allow air to flow through your items. Place a couple of chair cushions on top of the trunk, and place it at the foot of a bed or underneath a window for a decorative bench that serves double duty as secret storage.

- Use wide and flat plastic containers with wheels designed for under-the-bed storage.

- If you have available closet space, wrap a sheet around your out-of-season clothing to separate it from your regular inventory and protect it from dust. Attach the sheet with clips or clothespins.

- Store seasonal clothing in extra sets of luggage. Make sure to protect them from moisture, moths, and bugs, as listed in the following section.

Protecting your belongings

Make sure to choose a safe way to store clothing to protect it from the elements, as well as from pests and moisture. Below are a few suggestions:

- Place mothballs or scented cedar inserts in an old sock or glove so they do not touch the clothing directly. Mothballs can discolor your clothing, and they carry a strong odor that is difficult to remove. They are also toxic so make sure they are out of reach of children and pets.

- To absorb moisture and odors, place a small amount of scented cat litter in a sock, tying it at the top, and place inside your storage container.

- Lay items flat whenever possible to prevent wrinkling and tearing.

- Clean items before storing. Insects may be attracted to perspiration or any unseen drink or food spills.

- Stay away from storing items in a hot attic or cold basement. Extreme temperatures and light may damage your clothing.

- Do not store clothing around pipes that could burst or where water may gather.

- Keep containers off the floor where hidden moisture may be drawn.

- Use a dehumidifier in the area where your clothes are stored.

When focusing on closets around the home, there are other types of closets than just the ones found in your bedroom. Some of these closet spaces are often overlooked.

Coats, Linens, and Things

In many homes, the coat closet is the first you come to as you enter through the front door, which means it is the closet your visitors are most likely to see as well. Keeping it simple and as spacious as possible will allow you to use this space without fear of board games, gloves, and mittens spilling onto your guests when they open the closet door.

Coat closets

Organize your coat closet the same way you did with those in the bedroom. Pull everything out and start with an empty closet. Relocate any items that do not belong there. Vacuum it out completely, and wipe down shelves. Get rid of any coats or jackets your family no longer wears. *See Chapter 12 for additional information on clothing and coat drives.*

The following are a few suggestions for reorganizing your coat closet:

- Use plastic or wire S-hooks that fit over your hanging bar to hold umbrellas, tote bags, or scarves.

- If you have non-folding doors for this closet, hang a plastic shoe organizer on the door to hold hats, gloves, mittens, and scarves.

- Buy a bin, basket, or plastic drawer system that goes in the bottom of your coat closet. Cover when not in season so they are hidden and out of the way. A wicker or plastic picnic basket with a flip lid works well for this purpose because it is easy to open.

- Use a diaper stacker, which is a decorative item built to enclose stacks of disposable diapers, allowing easy access through the opening in the front. These hang over your closet rod, but have a big enough opening for your family members to reach in and grab what they need before heading out into the cold.

- Install stacking shelves at the bottom of the closet if possible.

- Assign a bin or basket, possibly in the color assigned to each member of your family, where each person can drop in the items they may want to bring outdoors, such as small toys, sidewalk chalk, flip-flops, or a jump rope.

- Nest smaller pieces of luggage inside larger pieces if you store your luggage in these areas.

- Hang full-length coats together at one end and place the shorter coats in the center for easier access to the shelving below.

Linen closets

Linen closets are normally narrow and offer little space. You may wish to use the sticky note game to determine what should be stored there and what should not. It is a good idea to remove any item not used for your bedding or bathroom areas.

Here are a few suggestions for keeping linen closets in order:

- Coordinate your extra sheet sets with the specific colors per bedroom, possibly even using the assigned colors for each family member. This way, you will always know which sheets fit a particular bed. For the guest room, you may prefer only white.

- Fold the sheets neatly, and store the matching pillow case inside the sheets to keep all the items together. This will also help keep the sheet sets clean and fresh smelling by keeping them contained until needed.

- Use the back of the door, if possible, to place a hanging organizer with see-through pockets to store smaller items, such as first aid items, razors, nail clippers, or napkin rings.

- Consider hanging table linens on trouser hangers if you have the closet space to spare. If not, roll them to eliminate creasing, and store in sets in plastic containers or baskets along with placemats, napkins, and table runners.

- Rather than folding towels, try rolling them and stacking them, similar to the way they are displayed at a spa. This prevents your stacks of towels from leaning, makes an attractive display, and makes it easy to grab a particular towel without disturbing an entire stack. Though it may require the same amount of space, it looks much better and is easy to arrange with larger towels on the bottom, smaller towels on top.

- Arrange towels by color, especially if you assigned each color to a member of your family.

- Use lower shelves to store extra rolls of toilet paper where smaller children can reach them.

- Store cotton balls, cotton swabs, bandages, or other frequently needed items in clear plastic containers with lids so the contents are always visible. If you cannot see it, you will not use it.

Games, crafts, and gift closets

If you have the luxury of a spare closet, then you can house all those pesky items that beg for space and take over your bedroom closets. These items are typically stashed in forgotten corners of your bedroom closets: wrinkled rolls of gift wrap or gift bags; bags of crushed bows; board games or jigsaw puzzles; or pipe cleaners and Popsicle sticks that may be needed for future school projects.

So, how do you go about organizing these items? First of all, if you do not have a closet that can store these items, purchase a free-standing cabinet or armoire with doors. The pull-out shelving and drawers keep everything hidden, yet provide a great work area.

Then, when organizing, try implementing the following tips:

- Purchase a gift wrap organizer. There are several products available, but Rubbermaid® offers one of the most versatile with separate pockets for tape, tags, pens, scissors, and other supplies. This holds up to ten rolls of gift wrap, and the entire organizer stores easily at the bottom of your closet.

- Shelves are vital. You will need as many as possible to keep this area organized.

- Stack games and jigsaw puzzles on lower shelves for easy access. Tell your children to make sure game pieces are always returned to their original boxes, or the games will no longer be used.

- Get plastic bags to store game pieces before returning them to their boxes. Once the boxes wear out or tear, move all pieces, along with the instructions, to clear, plastic stackable containers that are the size of shoe boxes. Fold and store the game boards underneath your stack of plastic boxes. Label each box and the matching game board.

- Store playing card sets in plastic bags, and place all the bags in one clear container. Keep specific directions for unique card games, such as Uno® or Rook, in the plastic bags.

- Place a check mark, specific shape, or a dab of nail polish on the back of puzzle pieces so they can easily be sorted when they are accidentally combined with another puzzle.

- Use clear, plastic, stackable boxes for storing similar items, such as glue sticks, scissors, or tape.

- Purchase containers designed simply for hobbies, making your supplies transportable. This works well for sewing, scrapbooking, quilting, and other such hobbies.

The next chapter will take you into the bedroom areas of your home. Following the tips in that chapter will ensure your bedroom can be a space for tranquility rather than a space where clutter grows.

Chapter 7

Bedrooms and
Broomsticks

Many parents give up on the condition of their kids' rooms as they face the ongoing tug-of-war trying to motivate them to keep the bedrooms clean. Tired of fighting the daily battle, they eventually concede by closing the door and hoping no one notices. Although it is important to prevent this clutter from becoming a daily battle, it is also important to instill good habits early on so that fighting clutter does not become a lifelong struggle for your kids. The best strategy to keeping the rooms clean is to only keep what is needed in there. If everything has a home, organizing belongings becomes much easier, and your kids will eventually learn to do this on their own.

Make sure the conversations you have with your kids are not always steered back toward the status of their bedrooms. And, whatever you do, never use cleaning as a punishment. If your children are sent to their rooms for doing something wrong and you tell them they cannot come out of their room until it is cleaned, inadvertently tying the two incidents together, it will ruin any chances of them ever helping you with this task willingly. Remember, your goal is for them to learn to manage themselves, and that can never happen if they are only forced to clean when they are in trouble.

In order for your kids to want to keep their rooms clean, they must have a reason to take pride in them. The atmosphere of their room needs to mean something to them, and they must enjoy spending time there. Allow them to choose their own theme or décor or even paint colors if repainting is an option. Have them design a mission statement strictly for their room so you can work together to meet their needs. Do they wish for a place to invite their friends? Do they want frequent sleepovers? Do they want an area strictly for reading books? Include their desires for their space in their mission statements, and then take that into consideration as you move toward uncluttering and reorganizing each room. Taking their ideas into account becomes even more important if your children share a room. They must respect each other's ideas, but it should still serve their own needs as much as possible.

CASE STUDY: DEANNA RADAJ, BANTE DESIGN

DeAnna Radaj
Bante Design LLC
904 W Eden Pl
Milwaukee WI 53221
deanna@bantedesign.com
www.bantedesign.com

DeAnna Radaj was once informed while in design school that she could never make a living by being an interior designer. But, after writing two

books, owning her own business, serving as a design consultant and host of her own radio show with an international listening audience through BlogTalkRadio, Radaj found a way to blend it all into a satisfying and busy career. Her books, the first one titled *Designing the Life of Your Dreams from the Outside In* and the second, *Feng Shui for Teens*, are available through Amazon®. Her radio show, *Feng Shui Fabulous*, is also available online at **www.blogtalkradio. com/bante-design-llc**.

Radaj's training includes degrees in both marketing and interior design, but she says she uses what she learned through her minor in psychology more than she ever thought when making design recommendations. When working toward her feng shui certification, she was exposed to the idea that where and how people choose to store their belongings has a great effect on their mental and physical well being.

Radaj's own philosophy on clutter is a blend of all she learned before. "Our stuff is the physical manifestation of our emotional baggage," she said. She helps her clients go through a clutter counseling process in order to permanently put that problem behind them. She makes a practice of interviewing all family members before making any recommendations to determine how the space is used, how often, and by whom.

"The key to making a space functional to match the lifestyle of a family is to understand what they have and how it is used," Radaj said. "My goal is to help them maximize the usage of the square footage they have to work with. I help families create space that is supportive of what they are trying to accomplish."

Radaj holds her clients responsible for their stuff, and for good reason. De-cluttering is a temporary solution, and unless you determine why it happens, the cycle will repeat itself. "I tell them, 'You bought it. You saved it. You collected it. You must deal with the reasons why you have it. If your stuff does not serve a positive purpose in your life right now, then it is holding you back and you must let it go.'"

Radaj makes a practice of completely taking the emotions out of dealing with stuff. "How can you say you love something that is piled in a corner in the attic?" she asked. Once her clients pick up on that perspective and identify how they want to use their space, they are guaranteed to find success at establishing an efficient household that offers positive energy for everyone who enters.

In their own beds

As you delve into your children's bedroom areas, understand that in order for them to take responsibility for their things in their room, they must learn to sleep in their own beds as early in life as possible. If they frequently start each night in your bed or sleep with a sibling, they will never feel as if they own their space. They know you, as a parent, will make up your bed, so it never crosses their mind they might need to do this on their own.

If your child struggles with sleeping in his or her own room, re-organizing and redecorating the room may be just the motivation he or she needs to embrace the idea of sleeping there once again. Allow him or her to set up a tent on the floor and sleep there for the night. Place glow-in-the-dark decals on the ceiling so he or she will look forward to the nighttime rituals. Play soft music at night, or listen to a favorite story that is recorded. Place a box fan in the room to add a little noise because sometimes the silence alone is what children fear the most.

Although you want your children's rooms to be a comfortable place for them to go, do not put so many things in a kid's room that there is never a need for him or her to join the rest of the family during activities and meals. Children need a place to call their own — to play, sleep, dress, and do homework. However, their room should never become a place that allows them to retreat on a regular basis, avoiding being around others.

Starting Seems to be the Hardest Part

Bedrooms should be a safe haven. Even adults long for a pleasant place to spend their time and find the peace to sleep at night. But, with any overwhelming task, the hardest part is to simply begin. The following ideas will soon provide everyone in your family a bedroom they are proud to call their own:

1. **Open the windows.** Because bedrooms tend to be darker rooms, let in some light to allow fresh air to enter. This is inspiring in and of itself. If you are cleaning at night, turn on all the lights, making it as bright as possible.

2. **Clear the floor.** Pull chairs, hampers, and anything that moves easily out of the room.

3. **Strip the beds.** Launder all bedding and toss pillows in the dryer for a few minutes on the tumble dry cycle. Turn the mattress. Vacuum underneath, and wipe dust off the headboard and footboard. Change bedding weekly.

4. **Dust the furniture.** Wipe everything down while it is empty, including the windowsill.

5. **Vacuum it thoroughly.** Do not forget the windowsills, ceiling fan blades, and top and bottom corners where dust and cobwebs gather.

6. **Remove all trash.** Check under the bed, behind dressers, desks, and bookshelves.

7. **Use a "Homeless" basket.** Get a laundry basket, and gather any item that goes in the bedroom but does not yet have an identified home. Use a separate basket for items that go in other rooms. Place the misplaced items in the basket so you are not frequently leaving your bedroom to put them in their correct location.

8. **Rearrange furniture.** Sometimes just a new layout works wonders. Place the chair by the window for reading, or turn the bed long ways to open more floor space.

9. **Unclutter the walls.** Too much of anything is distracting, causing the items you are trying to display to be overlooked.

10. **Wipe down walls.** The Magic Eraser by Mr. Clean works great to remove scuff marks and fingerprints.

11. **Find a home for everything.** Return books to shelves, file papers away, and limit the number of visible knickknacks.

12. **Label drawers or shelves.** Use sticky notes to label what goes in a particular drawer or shelf. By seeing what belongs there, it is much easier to determine what does not. You can leave the notes in place for a while if you are trying to teach your family the new locations of things, but

they need to be removed at some point or they become part of your clutter.

13. **Remake the bed.** A freshly made bed brightens any room. If your bedspread is reversible, flip it to the other side to try something new.

14. **Spray air freshener.** Take the time to notice the look, feel, and smell of a clean room.

What belongs in the kids' bedrooms

In order to determine what belongs in a child's bedroom, begin by listing items that do not belong in the room, including:

This is a good example of how to utilize space and organize your child's room. The shelves offer a way to organize a variety of things and are easily accessible. The computer desk is simple, and the cabinets under the shelves offer great storage.

- Your doll collection from when you were a child

- All the trophies you or your spouse acquired through the years

- Your book collection

- Your craft or hobby area

- Your gym equipment or hand weights

- Your record collection and antique record player, or any other sentimental items from you or your spouse's past

- Your family's computer

Keep the bedroom as simple as possible, with minimum furniture and maximum space, especially if your children share a room. Keep your children involved as you plan a space that is both functional and fun. For young children, you will only need the following items:

- Bed
- Toys
- Storage
- Clothes
- Desk — by age 4, try to provide a work area of their own, which will help them adjust as they begin their school years. Long before it is needed for actual school homework, they can draw, color, paint, make other crafts, and practice writing their numbers and letters.

Nightly checklist for kids

Remember you are asking for a six-week commitment from your kids, so set high standards early on. This is your chance to retrain them and teach them to better organize themselves. Once you have the closet organized, the rest of the bedroom should be easy to tackle. With a little attention each night, the bedrooms in your home will remain in much better shape.

Once your children's bedrooms are set up specifically for their needs, establish a routine that will carry your clutter-free family into its clutter-free future. Help them form a routine of keeping the room in order by writing a nightly "to-do" list on the mirror of your child's bathroom or dresser by using a dry erase marker, or print one out and place on a bulletin board. Allow them to make their own lists for their bedtime and morning routines, forcing them to think through the process of picking up after themselves. Some kids work well with a checklist that serves as a reminder, and this is a good way to demonstrate the responsibility that goes with having their own space. For example:

Tara's Nightly List
- ❑ Take a shower
- ❑ Put on pajamas
- ❑ Brush teeth
- ❑ Comb hair
- ❑ Wipe down bathroom sink
- ❑ Complete homework
- ❑ Put homework in backpack
- ❑ Put dirty clothes in hamper
- ❑ Put all trash in trash can
- ❑ Put toys in toy box
- ❑ Lay out clothes for the next day
- ❑ Give hugs
- ❑ Read book
- ❑ Go to sleep

The Magic of Children's Furniture

The brilliance of furniture available for kids' rooms is that it is inexpensive, colorful, versatile, and quite functional. Choose items that can grow with your child so you are not replacing furniture on a regular basis. Consider some of the following:

- For infants, purchase a crib that transforms into a toddler bed, and later into a twin bed.

- Look for infant furniture that serves several purposes. For example, you can purchase a bassinet that serves as a portable sleeper, bassinet, bedside sleeper, play seat, and changing table.

- IKEA offers a cubed shelving system called Expedit™ with optional doors in various colors so you can install them in a checkerboard fashion. This could be a great wall unit for any kid's room, and they would be thrilled to use it.

- Many companies offer a loft bed or bunk beds. The loft bed is a single bed with a chest of drawers or desk underneath. Some even come with decorative curtains or a tent for the area underneath the bed that transforms simple bedroom furniture into an imaginative play area.

- JCPenney offers the Allie Daybed, which hides a trundle bed underneath but gives the appearance of having drawers under the bed. Just slide it back in when you are done, and the room is neat and tidy.

- Look for furniture designed for dorm rooms where space is always at a minimum. A company called Dormco, which can be found at **www.dormco.com**, offers several futon sofas, including one that folds out in five different ways. It converts from a full-sized bed to a sofa, a loveseat, a lounger, and then folds up completely so it can be stored in compact spaces.

- A company called Waterful Wonderbeds has a division of children's furniture called Poggy's Kids, found at **www. poggyskids.com**, and they offer a creative Murphy wall bed that is decorated as a baseball locker unit on the outside and pulls down into a bed from the wall.

Uncluttering Your Kids' Stuff

Regardless of your children's ages, their own battle with clutter will continue until there is a specified home for each of their prized possessions. Using the same approach you used for entryways and closets, always consider vertical space to solve these problems.

- **Portable artwork** — Buy a carrying caddy for crayons, markers, coloring books, or index cards to take with you to appointments where your children will quickly grow bored. Ask the local pizza delivery company for a few small unused pizza boxes. These work great for creative moments in the car and can hold a few crayons or pencils and paper. Build the box inside out, placing the pizza logo on the inside, and have your kids decorate the outside. Stick some double-sided adhesive fabric tape inside to keep them closed, and you can even add a handle for easy carrying. Include a plastic baggie to hold a few supplies, and stick a piece of adhesive fabric material to the bag to hold it in place inside so it will not roll around or get lost. These can quickly be stored in your trunk when not in use.

- **Dolls, miniature cars, or action figures** — Store these in a carrying case with a handle as well. You may wish to purchase a case made for dolls or miniature cars, but for smaller collections, a simple caddy with a handle and a few foldout storage compartments should work just fine. Decorate the outside of each case with your child's name. This provides a permanent, yet mobile home for doll clothes and shoes. Take these to locations where they will be expected to sit quietly for longer times, such as the doctor's office or any time you have to run errands.

- **Designate a place to keep things that are packed and ready to go for the day** — Use either a specific hook or bench to store your children's items that are ready for the next trip out the door. When backpacks or lunchboxes are prepared for the next day, have your kids place these items in their assigned spot. This will keep them from losing items or leaving without them.

- **Managing play time** — Limit the number of toys your children can have out at one time. Have them put one away before taking out another, and clean up before moving onto the next activity.

- **Shelving** — Bookshelves work well in a child's room, if not overly crowded with books and other trinkets. Label each shelf and place a few items there, keeping a neat and tidy look. Decorate the back of each shelf with brightly colored fabric or contact paper to brighten the room. Store only what is needed or is important to your child on these shelves.

- **Sporting equipment** — Buy a sports tote bag and have it monogrammed with your child's name to store their gloves, shin guards, balls, bats, and any other equipment. They will carry their items with pride and will always know where their stuff is when leaving in a hurry for practice or games.

- **Stuffed animals** — An over-the-door shoe organizer with pockets works well for smaller stuffed animals. Or, try placing a toy hammock that hangs from the ceiling in the corner of your child's room. The reality of stuffed animals is they are cute but rarely used so allow them to be a room decoration.

- **Toys** — Your best bet for managing the clutter of toys is to maintain a certain inventory per room. Store unused toys in under-the-bed storage or in the basement or attic. Monitor what is being played with on a regular basis, and swap some around when they grow bored with a particular toy.

- **Toy boxes** — The solution to keeping toys tidy is a proper storage system. If you have a toy chest, place dividers inside so similar toys can be stored together. Or, use baskets that slide into shelving systems, and label the outside of those.

- **Window shelves for trophies** — Remember to use your wall space to add height to a room. Hang decorative shelves above your windows, and store your child's growing trophy or doll collection here.

Desk areas

Establish a good study area in your child's room so he or she can have a place to concentrate and the rest of the family can continue on with other activities. Your child needs his or her own space and supplies so he or she can concentrate and finish without interruption. Once you have a desk or table set aside for this purpose, make it kid-friendly with the following suggestions:

- Cut a piece of plastic glass to fit on the desktop. This will allow photos and notes to easily slide underneath for decoration but will keep the work surface free and clear.

- Buy a cork bulletin board, and hang it low enough on the wall for them to use it. Post a calendar there, marking their weekly schedule or any special events.

- Buy a hanging wall rack for magazines and notebooks beside the desk.

The Chest, the Drawers, and the Wardrobe

Bedroom spaces require storage. All dressers and drawers must have a well-defined purpose and a functional way to display their contents. Your drawer space should house organized stacks rather than unidentified rummage piles. To get this area in order, follow the steps below:

1. Empty every drawer. Although it creates a bigger mess in the beginning, there is a point to seeing all your items in one place. You can decide what still fits and what does not. You might realize you have 30 T-shirts, but you rarely wear them. As with your closet, get a donation bin and garbage can ready and quickly go through your items.

2. If an item has not been worn in the last year, get rid of it.

3. Wipe your drawers clean before returning any items.

4. Store only what is in season and used on a regular basis in your drawer space.

5. Consider inexpensive drawer dividers and organizing systems for each drawer, especially for drawers that contain smaller items like underwear and socks.

6. Categorize what each drawer will be used for. Give each drawer a label, and begin storing like items together.

7. Try rolling your T-shirts and filing them from front to back rather than stacking them. You can easily choose from each row without knocking the entire stack over. This works well especially if you have compartmentalized your drawers with smaller bins or organizers. Use long, fridge-pack drink cartons or juice box cartons as sorters by cutting off the tops.

8. Store smaller, matching items, such as socks or undergarments, together in plastic sandwich bags. This helps keep them together and is easy for packing.

9. For smaller children, you may wish to store complete outfits, including pants, shirts, socks, and underwear, in gallon-sized plastic bags within each drawer. Then, they can choose their own outfits each day.

10. Pay attention to what gathers naturally on top of your dresser, and designate a better spot for these items. For example, if you frequently drop loose change or rings there, find a small dish to hold these items.

Mentioning the unmentionables

As you go through your drawers, pay attention to your undergarments, and get rid of any items with holes or stretched out elastic. Place any panty hoses in sealed sandwich bags to prevent snagging on hooks, and file them upright in a small basket or box. Fold bras, one cup tucked in another, and file them in this fashion as well.

Cut down on your inventory of underpants. Dresser drawers are typically overstuffed with an extremely large collection of undergarments. Charities do not accept used underpants, so discard any underwear you do not wish to keep.

Sock wars

As discussed in Chapter 5, socks are a regular culprit in the problem of clutter in the home. But, as you store your new ones, try these ideas to better manage your sock situation:

- Keep a bag for unmatched socks in the laundry room. If you go two weeks without finding a mate, toss the spare one.

- For younger children, keep all paired socks together in larger zippered plastic bags. They will always know where to find them inside their drawer.

Jewelry

Not everyone in the family will have a large jewelry collection, but it helps to have a great system in place for those with jewelry.

Try the following suggestions to keep your jewelry piles manageable:

- Attach a tie rack to your wall. The best kind for jewelry is the type with a row of individual pegs. Hang necklaces or bracelets from the pegs. This keeps them from becoming tangled and makes them easily accessible.

- Slide slip-on bracelets or watches over a freestanding paper towel stand.

- Purchase a jewelry case with separate compartments for smaller rings and earrings.

- Use a plastic ice tray to hold sets of earrings inside a drawer.

- Use your jewelry to decorate the wall. For a large and colorful jewelry collection, design an area with hooks or nails, and display your collection prominently.

- For beginning jewelry earring sets for girls, store them using the cups from a foam egg carton. The ends can be stuck into the foam so they will not accidentally stick younger fingers. Store this safely inside a drawer.

- Use cloth-covered bulletin boards for hanging necklaces for young girls. Earrings can be stored here as well; just make sure they are well secured.

- Get a mesh fireplace screen, and hang all of your jewelry from this. It can become a decorative piece for your room.

- Hang hoop earrings over the edge of a wine glass.

- Get a hanging jewelry organizer with see-through compartments. Closet Organizer Kits offers one with 37 pockets that easily hangs in your closet. Find them at **http://closetorganizerskits.com/hanging-jewelry-organizer-black-37-pockets-organize.asp**.

Egg cartons and ice cube trays make organizing jewelry easy. Not only is your jewelry easily visible and accessible this way, but you can also group multiple pieces of jewelry together based on style or outfits you like to wear them with.

O
p
p
r
e
s
s
 t
h
e
M
e
s
s

Tip #7

Ten-minute Fix

Commit ten minutes per day to tidying up your own space, and have your kids do the same. Throw trash away; place dirty laundry in the hampers; return books to shelves; and place pens and pencils in designated containers. Do not allow stacks of papers to form. Soon, everyone will learn that cleaning their room is much easier because it should never take all day.

It is difficult to mention the bedroom areas without also covering the bathrooms so the following chapter will cover these heavily used areas.

Chapter 8

Bathroom Bingo —
Rules of the Game

Bathrooms are used constantly so they must be cleaned regularly and left in good shape for your family, as well as any houseguests. Even if you have the luxury of a private bathroom within your master bedroom suite, there are times when others may need to enter and use that restroom area. Bathrooms closest to the front door or family room require the deepest cleaning on a weekly basis because they will be used most often. A freshly cleaned bathroom is quickly ruined because of moisture, hairspray, splatters of water and toothpaste, and the most loathed of all cleaning responsibilities — the toilet areas. This chapter examines several ways to improve the set up, organization, and maintenance of your bathrooms.

Take Inventory of Supplies

If you have the benefit of several bathrooms in your home, you probably have no idea what is stored in the cabinets and drawers of these rooms. Pay attention to what items you find on the counters because those are normally the items used most often. Keep frequently used items in mind as you reorganize these areas. Get a trash bag, go from room to room, and remove anything that is old, almost empty, or unused, and place it in the trash. Old tubes of makeup, especially in liquid form, should be disposed of because they expire within six months of purchase. Nail polish hardens and becomes unusable after a couple of years so trash it.

As you go through each bathroom, get a large box, and place everything in it you plan to keep. Once your inventory of supplies is in one location, you can assess what you have, how it should be distributed, and where it is most likely to be used. Get a washcloth and wipe down all bottles and tubes, removing any stickiness or excess around the lids. You may find you have duplicates of items in various bathrooms.

Pay attention to which items need to be spread out among all the bathrooms in your house. Bandages and cotton swabs are used in every bathroom, so distribute them evenly in see-through containers. Each bathroom needs its own tube of toothpaste, extra rolls of toilet paper, air freshener, and facial tissues.

While your drawers and cabinets are empty, clean them thoroughly, making sure to remove any sticky spots. Spray antibacterial spray inside to kill germs and remove any musty odors. Leave the drawers and cabinets open to air out until you determine your need in each specific location. Sweep or vacuum the floors underneath, making sure to remove any stray hairs that tend to stick together in every nook and cranny of your bathrooms.

Remove all countertop clutter. Your counters need to remain clear, filled only with soap dispensers and toothbrush holders. If you keep them clutter-free, they are more likely to be cleaned and sanitized often. Once you determine what needs to be stored in each bathroom, it is time to organize.

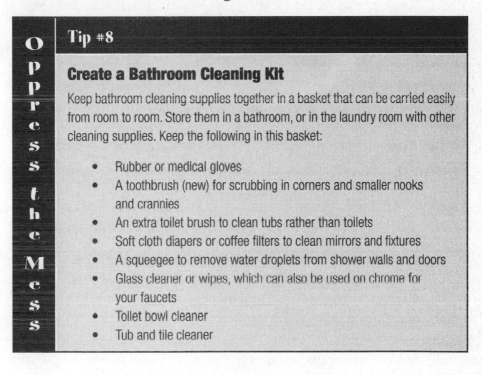

Tip #8

Create a Bathroom Cleaning Kit

Keep bathroom cleaning supplies together in a basket that can be carried easily from room to room. Store them in a bathroom, or in the laundry room with other cleaning supplies. Keep the following in this basket:

- Rubber or medical gloves
- A toothbrush (new) for scrubbing in corners and smaller nooks and crannies
- An extra toilet brush to clean tubs rather than toilets
- Soft cloth diapers or coffee filters to clean mirrors and fixtures
- A squeegee to remove water droplets from shower walls and doors
- Glass cleaner or wipes, which can also be used on chrome for your faucets
- Toilet bowl cleaner
- Tub and tile cleaner

Storing Items on Your Terms

Consider the following organizational ideas as you return the items to your cabinets and drawers:

- Discard all bar soap. It is messy to store and because talc is one of the main ingredients, it is more likely to cause a buildup of soap scum on your walls, shower curtains or doors, and tub. Replace with bottled soap and body wash.

- Keep dangerous medicines out of the medicine cabinets in the bathrooms your kids will use most frequently.

- Keep strong chemicals and cleaning supplies out of the kids' bathrooms as well. Store them elsewhere, and just leave packages of cleaning wipes for quick counter clean-ups instead.

- Consider labeling your shelves with masking tape or a label maker in the medicine cabinets or linen closets so everyone knows what goes on each shelf.

- Install racks made for sandwich bags and wraps inside your cabinet doors. These work great for holding shampoo bottles and lotions as well. .

- A round turntable, similar to one used in the kitchen, can be a great way to store taller bottles in your bathroom cabinets. You can turn until you reach what is needed rather than knocking everything else over when reaching toward the back to get an item.

- Make decorations out of items that are most used, and place them out in the open. For example, use a decorative basket for travel-sized shampoos, lotions, and conditioners. Cover tissue boxes with fabric to match the color of your towels or bathroom décor.

- Use drawer dividers for each drawer, and reserve the top drawers for items used most often.

- Store like items together. Shaving supplies go in one basket, hair supplies in another.

- Get a hanging rack for hair electronics. The hair dryer, straightener, curling iron, and accessories can hang neatly without cluttering your cabinets and drawers. Some are even designed to go inside your cabinet doors.

- Store hair supplies together in one basket. Brushes, combs, barrettes, and ponytail holders need to stay together. If you have a large supply of items, place them on a long ribbon off a hook or in your bedroom closet.

Wicker baskets provide a stylish and simple way to organize bathroom products. Use them under the sink or on a shelf.

- Place bobby pins and safety pins in a magnetic paper clip.

Weekly Bathroom Cleaning Tasks

Once you have your bathrooms in order, the responsibility follows to keep them that way. Consider the following schedule for cleaning and refreshing:

- Change hand towels twice a week, using an old one to wipe down the counter and sink area.

- Clean mirrors with glass cleaner. This works well on faucets and handles also.

- Clean and disinfect the toilet once a week, including any potty chairs your children use.

- Sweep and mop the bathroom floor, paying special attention to the corners and uncovered parts of the floor where hairspray and stray hair tends to stick.

- Clean your bath or tub with spray-on bathroom cleaner. Use an old toothbrush to scrub between tile areas and corners. Spray leave-on shower cleaner after each shower or bath to prevent the buildup of soap scum.

- Buy a squeegee to clean shower doors and walls.

- To clean mildew off shower curtains — either fabric or vinyl — remove them from the hooks and wash them with the laundry in hot water on the gentle cycle. Hang them to dry.

- Clean toothbrushes by soaking them in white vinegar or an antiseptic mouthwash.

Special solutions for not-so-special problems

In all bathrooms of your home, preventative measures must be taken at times so you are not caught off guard by the clogged up drain or rust stains that form around your drains and in the toilets because of hard water. Fortunately, the solution to these problems can be found many times in your very own kitchen.

At least once a month, perform the following tasks:

- For drains that are already clogged, use a couple of Alka-Seltzer® tablets then pour white vinegar down the drain. Wait a few minutes, then follow with hot water and your drain should run clear.

- For stubborn toilet-bowl stains, pour a can of cola into the bowl, and let it sit for an hour. Scrub and flush, and the citric acid from the cola product will dissolve your stains.

- For rust in sinks, tubs, or on counters, let a few drops of white vinegar or lemon juice sit for an hour and then scrub clean. You can also use white vinegar on mineral deposits or rust stains that develop around the seal of your faucets and fixtures.

- You may also pour 2 cups of white vinegar in your toilet bowls, and let it sit overnight, scrubbing in the morning. This should remove the stains rather than simply bleaching them away temporarily.

- Remove your showerhead, and allow it to soak in warm vinegar. Scrub with an old toothbrush to make sure all water openings are free of clogs. This will ensure your water pressure remains as high as possible.

- To remove soap scum from bathroom tiles and shower doors, dampen a dryer sheet and scrub. To keep soap scum from building back up, get a squeegee, and wipe down the walls and doors after showers are complete.

- If you have a whirlpool tub, fill it with warm water and 1 cup of bleach, then turn on the jets, and allow it to run its course. Run for about 30 minutes. To keep the jets clear and working properly, avoid using bubble bath and heavy bath oils.

- To prevent your mirror from fogging during showers or baths, clean with a mixture of water and dishwashing liquid. Repeat this as soon as you notice the mirrors fog-ging again.

- If a film develops on your mirrors because of frequent use of hair products, clean with a mixture of shampoo and water.

- To keep your bath mat from growing mold and mildew, hang it to dry after each use. Spray with tub cleaner dur-ing weekly cleanings and scrub, or wash in the washing machine and hang to dry. If it already succumbed to mold and mildew from past use, throw it away, and start all over. Never leave it in place for extended periods, espe-cially if it has suction cups underneath, because it will cause staining on your tub.

Becoming Master of the Master Bath

Bathroom storage cabinets, by default, become the temporary home of many of your unused and forgotten items. As in any bathroom, you may find an odd mixture of fancy skin-care prod-ucts, first aid items, nearly empty bottles, and tissue boxes. As you de-clutter, consider the following ideas:

- Throw out any liquid makeup, especially mascara and eyeliner, that is older than six months.

- Check all medicines and ointments for expiration dates, and discard the expired ones.

- Get baskets with handles for your daily care items, such as shaving accessories, combs or brushes, tweezers, den-tal floss, hairspray, or gel. Get a separate basket for those items belonging to your spouse. That way, when they are needed, each of you can pull your basket out. It is vitally important when sharing a bathroom to keep items separate but still easily accessible. This way, you are not fishing through stuff that is not yours when getting ready in a hurry.

- Store additional dental cleaning products in a similar basket, such as mouthwash and dental floss.

- Store cosmetics by category — face, eyes, lips, and nails — in small sorter drawers that can go either in your cabinet or rest on your counter.

- Create extra storage pace using a cabinet with shelves and doors that stand over the toilet. Decorate with candles, decorative boxes to hold extra soaps and shampoos, or wrap a folded hand towel with a ribbon.

- Store extra toilet paper in a 6-inch diameter cylinder vase, the perfect size for about four toilet paper rolls. At about 2 feet tall, it fits nicely beside the toilet. Tie a ribbon around the middle to dress it up a little.

- Take the top off empty cologne bottles, and wrap them in an old sock to place in your clothing drawers to serve as a sachet, which will make the contents of your drawer smell nice.

- If there is a linen closet for the master bath, use an over-the-door rack for hair dryers and other hair electronics or shavers. Wrap cords inside toilet paper rolls to keep them from getting tangled.

- Reconsider the number of bath towels everyone in your family owns. If you reuse them two to three times before washing, each person only needs three at the most to get through the week. Make sure they are hung to dry between uses so mold does not begin to form. Wash your bath towels more often if someone in the family has been sick and they share a bathroom with others. But, keep in mind that the linen closets in many homes are overstuffed with towels that are never used.

- Reserve top drawers of bathroom cabinets for items used on a daily basis, and use bottom drawers for less frequently used items.

- Install a shower caddy or hanging shelves that drain easily for shampoo and conditioner bottles.

- If you prefer baths as opposed to showers, consider an over-the-tub organizational caddy that holds your supplies just inside the tub, as opposed to sitting them around the edges, to keep your items within reach.

- There are several new products available for the shower, including shower radios, mirrors, and a company called The Droodle™ even offers waterproof notepads for jotting down quick ideas because many claim to do their best thinking while in the shower. For more information on this, visit their website at **www.thedroodle.com**.

- Install a double shower rod, using the inside bar for hanging towels to dry where they cannot be seen.

- Store a bathroom scale in your linen closet or underneath a shelving system. These come in handy but tend to get in the way.

Guest Bathrooms

Determine which bathroom guests will use most often. If you have only one bathroom, this is an easy decision, but if you have at least two, choose the one closest to the family room and front door to turn into your guest bath. This may only be a half bath, but it still needs to be set up in a welcoming fashion for your guests. If you have frequent overnight guests, choose the one that has a bath or shower and is closest to where they will sleep.

Try these suggestions for keeping your guest bathroom inviting, clean, and clutter-free:

- Decorate it nicely, hanging vibrant colored hand towels near the sink. Do not place only monogrammed or embroidered towels in there because your guests may be afraid to use them.

- If the room is small, you can make it welcoming by hanging pictures or placing candles around the sink or on the back of the toilet. Leave a candle lighter out of the reach of smaller children if you do not mind your guests actually using the candles for relaxation purposes.

- Make sure the guest bathroom is cleaned weekly, including the mirror. Clean the bathroom more often if your family members use it on a regular basis.

- Store extra toilet tissue underneath the sink or on a stand in the bathroom so they do not run out at inopportune times.

- Place a small wastebasket in there that matches the color of your décor. Line the wastebasket with either a plastic grocery bag or small trash bag so if the trash becomes full while your guests are present, it can quickly be gathered, tied together, and taken out.

- Place matching hand soap and lotion dispensers beside the sink.

- Provide a can of room deodorizer spray and a box of tissues on the back of the toilet.

- If this room does have a bath or shower and overnight guests will use it, keep extra travel-sized sets of shampoo, soap, and razors in a basket under the sink or in the linen closet.

- Place an over-the-door hook with multiple pegs for robes or clean clothes.

- For extended stays, keep extra nail clippers, toothpaste, aspirin, antacids, talcum powder, bandages, and antibiotic ointment in a medicine cabinet, drawer, or closet in case needed.

- Establish a hamper or bag for the dirty clothes of your guests. They may wish to launder their own clothes but still need a private location to keep them until they can be cleaned.

- Keep a plunger in a basket made for plants, complete with an inner waterproof liner, beside the toilet area. The basket provides a place to return a wet plunger after use. A small wastebasket can work for the same purpose.

- Make sure there is a bath mat outside the bathtub or shower so the floor does not get wet, possibly causing your guests to slip.

- Keep an extra box of feminine hygiene products in an inconspicuous location but readily accessible in case it is needed.

Rules for the Kids' Bathroom

Most parents make it a practice to regularly pick up after their kids. While it is all right to do this on occasion, your goal during this six-week period is to retrain yourself, as well as retrain your children, to be more involved in maintaining the home — primarily their bedrooms and bathrooms.

In the bathroom your kids use on a regular basis, remove as many items as possible so there will be no distractions or extra clutter. Then, take a weekend to begin the following practices:

1. Clean the entire bathroom, showing them that many of the tasks can be done quickly and easily. Leave a pack of antibacterial wipes under the sink so your kids can quickly wipe down the sink and counter in the future. You might also include some glass cleaner wipes, as they are a quick way to touch up your mirrors. Kids think it is fun to use the wipes and will do so if they are readily available.

2. Buy new toothbrushes, color coordinated to your child's assigned color. Replace them after any child becomes ill, or every three months. Do not store toothbrushes where they are touching each other to prevent the spread of germs and bacteria.

3. Hang a towel and washrag in each of their assigned colors.

4. Make sure you have enough towel racks or hooks for them to hang towels to dry when they are done showering. This system works best if each person has their own hook. If

you are short of towel bars, consider an over-the-door rack with multiple hooks.

5. Make sure they know what day of the week laundry is done and when towels need to be placed in their colored hamper. If they go more than a week without placing their towel in the hamper, or if you find it on the floor rather than on their assigned hook or rack, you may need to remove it for the time being and allow them to run out of towels in their bathroom. Give them a reason to change this behavior.

6. Place extra rolls of toilet paper under the sink, and make sure they know how to change the roll.

7. Get a small basket in each child's assigned color to store their belongings under the sink or in a drawer. Then, they can pull their basket out when using those items and quickly return it when finished.

8. Your kids may think it is fun to use travel-sized bottles of shampoo and soap so they can each have their own. For younger kids, this may be a great way to introduce them to using their own bottle, managing how much to use, and it is not a huge deal if they let it all spill out into the shower. If you choose to use the smaller bottles for a while, buy extras, and place in their colored baskets.

9. Have them take turns wiping down the sink and counter at least once during the week. Or, assign one child to take out the trash while the other wipes down the sink. They may need your assistance cleaning toilets, bathtubs, and showers properly, but they still need to be involved with the daily upkeep of the bathroom they use most often.

10. Follow your own system. It is all right to check their progress but not to clean the bathroom while they are away. Find a way to make it part of their routine, or add it to their checklist.

11. Choose a short-term reward if they get through the first week and the bathroom is in good shape. It can be something as simple as going to see a movie or taking them to their favorite restaurant, but keep them motivated, and give them a reason to succeed.

12. For younger children who still play with toys during their bath time, get a mesh carrier that zips, and hang it from suction cups above the tub. This will allow the items to dry and the water to drain down. Let your child put the toys away after bath time.

13. Instruct them to notify an adult as soon as possible if their toilet gets stopped up. It is wise not to allow them to use a plunger before they are ready, and many kids ignore the problem, which makes it worse in the long run. Help them understand the purpose for the plunger, and that a stopped up toilet just happens at times. If a child causes a toilet to overflow, they may become afraid to even flush it again the next time so keep this in mind when discussing this issue.

Cosmetics — the price of beauty and where to store it all

As cosmetics enter your home, there are a few things to keep in mind.

1. Most items are small and can get lost easily.

2. Liquid cosmetics usually expire within six months, and powdered cosmetics expire within a year.

3. Cosmetics should never be shared because germs are easily spread in this way.

4. Use brushes to apply makeup and never your finger, which adds to the build up of bacteria.

5. Wash brushes and applicators monthly using a touch of shampoo and warm water. Allow them to dry completely before storing again.

6. All makeup should be stored in a cool, dry place. If stored in the bathroom, it must be in a moisture proof container.

There are many creative and functional ways to store cosmetics. Because they should not be shared, each user must choose his or her own method of storage and organization. Consider the following ideas as you determine what best serves your purposes:

- Purchase a caddy with handles, small fold out compartments, and a mirror so it can be taken wherever needed.

- Plastic six-drawer organizers can hold all of your cosmetics, with one drawer for eyes; one drawer for lips; one drawer for clippers and tweezers; and so on. These can be stored on a linen closet shelf or in your cabinets.

- Skin-care items, such as moisturizer, makeup remover or cleanser, and lotions, can go in a separate caddy or basket but need to be stored together as well.

- Buy a magnetic board designed to hold pencils and supplies inside school lockers. These can hold eye and lip pencils, makeup brushes, and even cotton swabs or cleaning cloths. Hang it in your bathroom, closet, or closest to the mirror you use when applying makeup.

- Cutlery trays work great inside drawers for storing smaller items by category.

- An expandable travel bag that rolls up when not in use can be hung on the back of the door. These come with several compartments and make your cosmetic stash as portable and neat as possible.

- Desk caddies designed to stand up scissors and pens on top of desks can work well. Buy one that rotates so you can quickly access what you need.

By finding a way to store your cosmetics, you will use what you have, prevent yourself from accidentally buying duplicates, and will find that for the women in your home, being beautiful is as much fun as it looks.

The next chapter will examine ways to reign in the busiest room of the house: the kitchen.

Chapter 9

Cutting the
Kitchen Chaos

T hough the purpose of your family room is to hold family get-togethers, the truth is that families tend to gather most often in the kitchen. Your family will spend a great deal of time in your kitchen, whether they are reaching for a quick snack or drink or gathering for a family dinner. Even the neighborhood friends will come and go freely as they grow more comfortable in your home.

Your kitchen requires even more attention than your closets, bedrooms, or family room because it will become cluttered on a daily basis — perhaps even on an hourly basis. It is impossible to ignore the kitchen and the daily work that comes with it. For this reason, it is best to embrace the role this room plays as it brings your family together. The kitchen becomes the place where most communicating is done and special memories are created. The smells that waft through the house draw your family to your kitchen, anxious to see what tasty surprises will soon follow.

Open for Business, and When to Close

The truth is that parents spend most of their cleaning time in the kitchen. With meals, snacks, late-night desserts, and school lunches, the kitchen becomes cluttered and dirty again within minutes after it is cleaned. Sharing responsibilities and rotating them from child to child is difficult during the school week with their homework, team practices, and earlier bed times so it is safe to assume that much of the kitchen care will fall on the parents.

For this reason, consider the idea of closing your kitchen at a certain time of night. Once the dishes are cleaned, dishwasher is running, lunches are made for the following day, sink and counters are wiped down, and floor swept each evening, it is usually late at night and nearing bedtime. Announce to your family the kitchen is closed for the night because the last thing you need is for someone to dirty another dish or leave a half-eaten cookie on the counter. Close the kitchen so it will remain in good shape to start the next day.

Refrigerator Magnets — Limiting the Pull of the Refrigerator on Your Family

If a closet is an area used for storage that has its own door, then your refrigerator may be the most used "closet" in your home. Frequently opened and closed, the contents inside are more visible than those of your other closets. It draws your family toward it, pulling them like a magnet with each trip through the kitchen. For this reason, your refrigerator has to be more organized, more functional, less cluttered, reserved only for what you will use, and cleaned out more often. It requires attention on a weekly basis.

CASE STUDY:
AUDREY CUPO,
A BETTER SPACE

Audrey Cupo, Professional Organizer
A Better Space
Jamison, PA
betterspace@comcast.net
www.4abetterspace.com
(215) 491-5193

Audrey Cupo says she has been naturally organized her entire life, a talent that serves her well. After 23 years as a paralegal, she decided to open her business, A Better Space, in 2004. She specializes in residential organization, as well as time and paper management systems. Audrey feels that she has a unique perspective to offer her clients as her life experiences have taken her through being a widow at an early age, raising a special needs child, being a divorcee, and eventually, an entrepreneur. Audrey has consistently found a way to rise above her circumstances, and she helps her clients do the same. She thrives on recognizing the potential in any situation, no matter how difficult it seems at first.

Passionate about keeping items out of landfills, Audrey is an advocate of recycling. She gets a thrill out of taking items her clients already own and repurposing them in some way. By donating to local charities rather than throwing items away, she finds that her clients are more likely to part with their belongings.

The largest obstacle Audrey sees for families trying to make improvements in their living situations is the lack of a long-term commitment. If they seek a quick fix, they are less likely to see it through until the end. The key to the success for any family is their own desire to change and maintain their own system afterward.

"When everything has a place, it is easy to maintain," Audrey said. "It's never too late to learn to be organized, and children learn by example. So, if you want your children to be more organized, they need to see their parents being more organized as well."

She recommends using Space Bags to take large, bulky clothing and shrink them down to store in smaller spaces using the vacuum cleaner to pull the excess air out. It also protects from moisture, unwanted pests, and musty odors. She prefers wire clothes hangers covered with velvet because they are thinner than the plastic ones and keep clothes from sliding off, though they are not great for heavier items such as coats or suits. To conserve energy, Audrey recommends plugging electronics into power strips and turning them all off when not in use.

For meal planning, she offers her own U-Can-Do-It Grocery Shopping Checklist, a comprehensive list arranged by category so you just check off what you need from the store. Many of her clients laminate this list and use it repeatedly. She also recommends creating meal plans and grocery lists at the same time each week. By looking for recipes that work in a slow cooker or those that take less than 30 minutes to prepare, meals become less chaotic.

"Once you are at the grocery, divide your list among your older kids and get the job done quickly. Keep a cooler in the car for frozen and refrigerated goods, and carry the cooler in as soon as you get home," she said. "That way, the rest of the groceries can be brought in later if you are crunched for time."

Audrey says the best part of her career is seeing the lifestyles of her clients transform before her own eyes. By reclaiming their homes, they are also able to reclaim their time and energy, reserving a few spare minutes each week to take care of themselves in the process.

Cleaning out your refrigerator

Here are a few steps for cleaning out your refrigerator:

- Choose the day before your trash is scheduled for pick up to take on this daunting task. You do not want leftover food spoiling in the trash can in your yard or garage for any length of time.

- Get a cooler with some ice packs to store your refrigerated items until you can return them to the refrigerator.

- Consider cleaning out your fridge the day before you do major grocery shopping, as your supplies are dwindling.

- Prepare a sink of very hot water with dish soap in advance for the plastic containers you will rescue from your refrigerator.

- Pull the trash can over to your refrigerator. Start with any dish covered in plastic wrap or tin foil. Scrape out the contents, and immediately drop the dish in your sink of hot water.

- Toss the take-home boxes or bags from restaurants in the trash.

- Check for any dried out food items, such as partially opened lunch meat or unused produce, and throw these away.

- Check for expiration dates on all items. Even those that are unopened may be expired and risky to eat. Take note of items that go unused, and choose not to buy them again. Read more about expiration dates later in this chapter.

- Remove everything from your refrigerator. Rinse and wipe down all jars and containers to remove any stickiness. Get rid of duplicate containers of food — your family does not need three jars of grape jelly.

- Clean the shelves and drawers in your refrigerator until they shine. Clean from the top down, making sure to even clean underneath the sliding drawers at the bottom. Wipe down the walls and top of it as well. Use a spray that smells great and fights germs and bacteria.

- Clean the vent or kick plate underneath your refrigerator door, where the refrigerator meets the floor. You can feel air blowing from the vent underneath at times. Spills often go unnoticed here, and dust gathers easily.

- Remove all items from the front and side of your refrigerator so you can clean them, too. Wipe down the water and ice dispenser if you have one. Clean the edges of the door gasket that seals your refrigerator shut, using a toothbrush to get in between the folds where spills sometimes hide.

Now what?

It is time to place your items back in the refrigerator, but this time, with a well-designed plan. Here are a few things you need to know before returning your perishables to their rightful home. Following the steps below can assist you greatly as you reconstruct your refrigerated storage plan from scratch.

- The coldest part of your refrigerator is normally near the freezer because it pulls cool air from the fan in the freezer. If you have a side-by-side unit, the fan is still near the top. The door is the least chilled area, followed by the area where crisper drawers are usually located at the bottom. Keep this in mind as you determine where to store things.

- As with your closets and bedrooms, remember to keep items your kids need low and easily accessible.

- You may wish to purchase heavy-duty, see-through containers with strong lids to store your items, grouping similar items together, such as cheeses or lunch meats.

- Use your crispers at the bottom to store salad items, lunch meats, and healthy snacks. The crisper drawers are designed to control humidity rather than temperature so keep this in mind when finding a new home for your food items.

- Keep a close eye on fresh produce, and store it where it can be seen easily. Do not purchase produce unless you have plans to use it within the week. It spoils easily and sometimes is forgotten.

- Group condiments together, perhaps in the door. Place taller ones behind shorter ones, and make sure all are visible. Throw away any duplicates.

- Assign a purpose for each shelf: drinks on one shelf, dairy on top, and covered containers of food in the middle.

- Store older items close to the front where they will be used first. This works for eggs, sour cream, or milk.

- Clean out your fridge quickly before heading back to the grocery. It is the only true way to know exactly what you need and what you still have plenty of.

Expiration dates

A great way to unclutter your kitchen and become more organized in the process is to search your cabinets, refrigerator, and freezer for expiration dates on food. Notice the difference between an actual expiration date and a "sell by" date that is used by the merchandiser. The dates listed serve as guidelines for quality rather than safety. As you check your own inventory of food, it is a great way to determine what items are used regularly and what products should no longer be purchased. If it was not used before the expiration date, it probably does not need to be replaced.

Though some items remain good for a few days after the expiration date passes, dairy products may occasionally sour prior to their expiration dates. Pay attention to the smell, texture, and appearance of items as you open them. A parent is much more likely to notice this than a child who may be preparing his or her own snack so plan to do this on a weekly basis.

For those items that do not recommend a specific date, such as fruits and vegetables, squeeze to test freshness, or check for odd sliminess or scent. Fresh produce has a shorter shelf life so buy as needed rather than buying large amounts in advance.

Avoiding Freezer Burn

Your freezer may need to be cleaned out less often than your refrigerator, but do not ignore it. Never assume all items in your freezer are still good because they are frozen. Freezer burn takes a toll on partially opened packages, and though it does not affect the safety of your food, it changes the texture by making it dry or tough to chew in spots. This can be detected by the presence of ice gathering inside the packaging of food. If items were allowed to thaw at one point and have been refrozen, they most likely have freezer burn.

Follow these steps to clean out your freezer:

1. You may wish to briefly turn off the refrigerator, either at the breaker box or by unplugging it. This will keep your

washrag from sticking to the sides and help you better clean inside.

2. Store items in a cooler while you work.

3. If your ice sits for a long time, throw it out, and start fresh as, it can absorb odors or other items that may splatter or leak on the ice when placed in the freezer. Wash ice trays. If you have an icemaker, turn it on again as soon as your tray is in place.

4. As with the refrigerator, wipe down everything, including the door gasket.

5. Clean all shelving.

6. Turn the unit back on.

When returning items to your freezer, try these steps:

1. Store rectangular boxes on a shelf like books. Make sure you can easily read all labels.

2. Place ice cream and larger items on bottom shelf where there tends to be more room available.

3. Keep similar items together, such as meats, snacks, and vegetables.

4. For smaller items, such as ice packs, burritos, or ice cream sandwiches that fall out easily, get a covered see-through container or zippered plastic bag to store these.

5. Store bagged vegetables in the door, folding them so they can line up easily and the labels are visible from the outside.

Cabinet Creations

As with most storage space, no family claims to have enough cabinet space in their kitchen. But, the typical family also increases their collection of stuff until it fills whatever cabinet space they have to offer. It is not necessary to keep plastic tumblers from every ballgame attended or have a collection of 24 souvenir coffee mugs. You must value your space and use every inch of it for good purpose.

A few things to keep in mind as you conquer your cabinets:

- Avoid using contact paper or shelf paper on shelves or in drawers. It is not allowed in restaurant settings because it actually draws bugs by giving crumbs a place to hide underneath the paper.

Under-the-counter shelving systems such as this allow you to utilize space and organize your pots, pans, and their lids.

- You can reorganize one cabinet at a time, but it may be necessary to do them all at once so you can better choose where items should be stored.

- Store items on the kitchen table, or somewhere away from your counter space, keeping them clear so you can wipe down all the shelves above them.

- Get a step stool and thoroughly clean all shelves in your cabinets, including the tops of them. Wipe down splatters from the outside of doors.

- Wipe off any sticky jars or containers.

- Pull a small trash can up to your counter to dump your crumbs or salt and pepper particles.

- Scrub the cabinet corners well.

- Clean areas underneath the cabinets where grease or other items from the stove or sink may splatter.

- If you see any signs of bugs or droppings from rodents, notify your exterminator. It may be wise to keep the cabinets clear until they are sprayed and you can wipe them down again.

- Use this opportunity to clean your stovetop and burners, as well as the drawer underneath your oven.

Enhancing your available space

Before returning your items to the cabinets, do as much as possible to expand your available cabinet space with some of the following ideas or gadgets.

- Purchase a Lazy Susan, a circular tiered rack that rotates so you can see all items. This works well for storing spices and smaller items.

- For deeper cabinets, try placing a cardboard mat, similar to those found in the bottom of cases of water or drink cartons, on the shelves. This will help you scoot items closer as needed without scratching the surface of your shelves.

- For deeper and taller cabinets, install two pull-out shelves on wheels to maximize this space. Organize-It offers several of these products from their website at **http://storage. organizeit.com/storage/roll-out%20shelves**.

- Buy expandable shelf organizers, which are tiered racks that stand on shelves and expand to fit the width of your cabinet. This is perfect for storing smaller items that tend to get lost behind others. You can find them online at The Container Store at **www.containerstore.com/shop/ kitchen/cabinetOrganizers/upperCabinets?product Id=10023942**.

- Use door racks to store sandwich bags and foil wraps.

- Group items together in a bin or basket that can be pulled out easily.

- Install wire under-shelf baskets that hang from your shelves to hold cup lids or squeeze bottles. The Container Store also offers these at **www.containerstore.com/shop/ kitchen/cabinetOrganizers/upperCabinets?product Id=10000700**.

- Use an over-the-sink shelf to store soap dispensers and other items that need to stay dry.

- Install a pull-out shelf under the sink to hold your trash can so it is easier to access.

- Many organizers are designed for storing everything from dish towels to pots and pans. Measure your cabinet space, and see what is out there. Even one of these products that converts unusable space to usable space is worth it.

- Get a standing pot lid rack, similar to a dish rack, to store lids for pots and pans in a cabinet rather than cramming them into the drawer underneath your stove. Lids to your pots and pans are bulky, difficult to store, and it is hard to find the right size when you need them. This rack should solve these problems. Organize-It offers one that stores up to nine lids at a time.

- Install a paper towel holder underneath a cabinet or inside a cabinet door under the sink to free up valuable counter space.

Rhyme and reason — placing things where it makes sense

Once you have your cabinets all cleaned out and their contents spread out in disarray before you, it is time to rethink your kitchen. Group items together as you decide where to store them. Follow these suggestions as you determine your new system of storage:

- Take note of what is used in a particular area, and store it there.

- Store the cooking utensils near the pots and pans.

- Store flat bake ware underneath the oven.

- Keep spices, oils, and other cooking supplies near the stove.

- Place cups closest to the refrigerator.

- Unless they are duplicate items, avoid stacking items in your cabinets. It causes them to be difficult to find, reach and access.

- Place sticky notes on each cabinet door to show what is in each until your family learns the new system.

Steering clear of the junk drawer

The top drawer that is most available as you enter the kitchen becomes the easiest place to store any stray items left around the kitchen. This drawer may be an interesting mixture of pencils, pens, notes, cards, and even a small screwdriver or hammer. Choose from these tips to help you organize your drawer space and to prevent a junk drawer from growing.

- Buy a wide or expandable silverware tray or organizer for every drawer. They work great for storing scissors, pens, rubber bands, chip clips, or twist ties.

- Get two wide and flat trays for storing larger kitchen utensils, such as spatulas, ladles, and stirring spoons.

- Purchase a hanging utensil rack for larger and matching cooking utensils, such as spatulas, ladles, whisks, and even your smaller pans. Hang this against the wall beside your stove.

- Do not store leftover condiment packets in your drawers. They burst easily and attract critters as well. If you must keep them, store them in the refrigerator in an enclosed bag or container.

- Store cookie cutters and other bulky items seldom used together in a see-through plastic container. Remove them from your drawer space completely.

- Hang oven mitts if possible.

- Rather than having a drawer of dish towels, get a rack that hangs on the inside of a cabinet door or a over-the-door rack that simply slides on.

Tip #9

O
p
p
r
e
s
s

t
h
e

M
e
s
s

Where to Store Kitchen Items

Organizing your kitchen may begin with pulling everything out of your cabinets. Though this initially creates a bigger mess, you can begin to evaluate what you have, what you need, and where to keep it.

1. Store similar items together. Canned goods go with canned goods; boxed cereals go with breakfast items; and baking goods and spices are stored together.

2. Store daily dishes and flatware in the most accessible place for your family. Make it easy for your children to help themselves.

3. Create centers. Store items used for preparing food closest to where the food is prepared. Dishes go closest to the sink or dishwasher. Baking pans go near the stove and baking goods.

4. Devise a method that makes sense. As you solicit the help of your family on a regular basis, remember that they are less likely to put items away if they are not sure where they belong.

Pantry Progress

If you are fortunate enough to also have a pantry for food storage, this provides a home for all of your non-perishable food items, freeing your cabinet space for dishes.

As with every other project you tackled, you must begin by pulling everything out of your pantry. Clean it thoroughly, making sure to wipe down shelves and to sweep the floor. Follow these steps as you reorganize your pantry:

1. As you evaluate each item, determine when you last used it, and decide if it is still needed. Toss out any partially opened items as they have most likely grown stale.

2. If an item did go unused for a long time, determine the reason. Was it because it was not visible, or was it because your family did not need it?

3. Because canned goods have a long shelf life, donate any canned goods that are neglected or unused for an extended time to a local food bank. Check the expiration date to ensure the food is still good to eat, but if your family has not eaten it by this point, they most likely will not.

4. Relocate potato chips, cookies, or crackers to plastic bags or stackable, clear containers with lids to preserve freshness. Label them with expiration dates as you dispose of their original packaging.

5. Assign a shelf for similar items. Canned goods can go on the bottom shelf, and lunch items go on the next shelf. Snacks like cookies, crackers, and chips go on the next one, and cereals on top. Arrange them where they need to be so your kids can reach them.

6. Store pet food in airtight containers in a crate or tub on the floor underneath your shelves, placing all pet items in that one crate. These keeps them out of sight, prevents the food from getting stale, and ensures your pet supplies do not take over the kitchen or laundry room.

7. Use a door rack to hold trash bags or other wraps.

8. Buy a wire soup rack that holds soups sideways and rolls the next one down as needed. This can work well for canned drinks in the refrigerator as well.

9. Label each shelf so your family returns items to the proper shelves.

10. Go through the pantry when making your grocery list. Toss what has expired or needs disposal, and replace them as needed.

Electronic appliances

Each holiday season begins with the greatest new inventions that claim to dice, slice, grill, and help you prepare food better than before. They are designed to make great gifts so chances are that many found a way into your kitchen. But, each appliance has a few things in common: They are bulky, difficult to store, take up valuable counter space, and unless they are used often, vital parts scatter and are difficult to find when needed. So, keep what appliances are needed, and donate the rest.

- If an appliance is not used, remove it from your kitchen. Donate unused items to charity, and trash the ones that no longer work properly.

- Store appliances that are used more frequently in lower cabinets where you have space available.

- For any other appliances you do not use regularly, store them above the cabinets in an orderly fashion.

- Wrap the cords either in a toilet paper roll or with rubber bands or twist ties to prevent them from becoming tangled.

- Purchase an appliance garage, which is a cabinet just for appliances offered by many companies for less than $150. An appliance garage creates space by fitting between your top and bottom cabinets, even stretching into the corners. It has a roll down door, similar to that of a garage. It creates a place to "park" your appliances permanently. You can buy it in wood to match your cabinets. It is a nice addition to any kitchen décor, even if you must sacrifice a little counter space in order to install it. Kitchen Source offers one that takes advantage of unused space in the corners at the following link: **http://www.kitchensource.com/cau/na-appliancegarage.htm**.

Kid-proofing your kitchen

Your goal as your children get older is to teach them to help by putting away dishes or groceries. In some ways, it makes sense to store items where your children can reach them. However, for children up to age 3, and sometimes even older, you will need to childproof your kitchen so there are no dangers to them. Consider these suggestions for doing so:

- Place cabinet latches on doors and drawers where cleaning products or knives are stored.

- Reset the temperature on your hot water heater to no more than 120 degrees to prevent scalding at all faucets in your home.

- Use safety plugs or outlet covers.

- Supervise small children in the kitchen at all times.

- Do not leave pet dishes out where small hands can turn them over or even sample their remaining bits of food.

- Reorganize the kitchen, placing items that present potential danger on higher shelves out of reach of tiny hands.

- Buy childproof caps for everything, including the nozzles on cleaning products that can be placed in a locked position.

- Never remove a dangerous chemical or cleaning product from its original container and place it in your own container because you may forget what you placed in the new container. Someone in your family may mistake the contents for water or something harmless and get sprayed in the eyes or mouth by accident.

- Do not use tablecloths. Tiny hands can pull them, heaping everything from glass dishes to sharp knives on top of them.

- Install a child safety gate to the entrance of your kitchen so your child is never in that room unsupervised.

CASE STUDY: SANDRA EINSTEIN, E=MC² ORGANIZING & COACHING CONSULTANTS, INC.

Sandra M. Einstein,
chief efficiency officer
e=mc² organizing & coaching
consultants, Inc.
ADD LIB Coaching
781 Village Circle
Gates Mills, Ohio 44040
emc2org@mac.com
www.emc2organizing.org

Though her company has been in business since 1996, Sandra Einstein's varied work experiences range from serving as a third-grade teacher to selling educational books to retail sales and management. Though much of her organizational skills came naturally, she admits that each of her previous career skills make her better at her current profession as an organizer. Through teaching organizational skills to 8 and 9 year olds, she learned to simplify the process. As a sales representative for educational materials, her vehicle served as her office so she kept client files easily accessible and a ready inventory with her at all times. She sharpened her business management and merchandising skills through her experience in retail, serving as the manager at a women's clothing store.

Einstein encourages her clients to donate clothing rather than to sell it through a consignment shop because the cost of dry cleaning the items in advance often costs more than the small profit they would make on the sale of the clothing itself. She does, however, recommend reselling furniture and household goods. For high dollar items, she collaborates with a local company that appraises valuables and organizes estate sales.

Einstein finds herself offering the following advice to new clients most often: "Be patient with yourself. Clutter does not happen overnight and neither will the clean up. One of my mantras is this," she said. "Complete the task at hand. Finish one room before tackling another."

$E=mc^2$ serves a large number of clients who exhibit certain disorders, such as attention deficit disorder, bipolar disorder, obsessive compulsive disorders, and even some with hoarding issues. For these individuals and their families, it is vitally important to maintain a structured environment with as few distractions as possible. Though it takes a typical individual 30 days to create a new habit, Einstein says it takes 60 to 90 days to accomplish this feat if any of the disorders mentioned above become a factor. Because children with ADHD tend to be forgetful and naturally disorganized, use visual charts with pictures to remind them. She recommends keeping it as simple as possible, and making sure these kids get positive feedback. Help them think through their day in advance, making sure their homework is ready to turn in and inside their backpack. Allow them to choose their own clothing for school, and keep the same schedule as much as possible.

For families where both parents work outside of the home, when time at home to organize is limited, Einstein recommends always putting things away immediately. "Do not allow your children to throw, drop, or toss coats, papers, clothing, mail, toys, purses, and shoes. Once each item has a designated home, make sure those items are placed there as soon as your family walks through the door," Einstein said.

For larger families where many family members share space, such as bathrooms, she advises them to share bath products as much as possible. Fewer shampoo bottles and tubes of toothpaste mean less clutter in this area.

If e=mc^2 could design homes specifically for families, they would all have a walk-in pantry off the kitchen area with shelving space deep enough to house small kitchen appliances, as well as non-perishable items purchased in bulk.

Dishing it Out

Dishes require immediate attention after they are used. Leaving them dirty will make your job much harder. Most homes are equipped with a dishwasher to assist with this task, but it must be unloaded and ready for action following meals.

Dishwasher cycles

Even with small families, you will most likely use your dishwasher on a regular basis, normally several times a week. Try establishing the following rules for your family:

- Never place dishes in your sink while food is still on them. Teach your kids how to scrape their plates off and slide the food into the trash or garbage disposal.

- Make sure all dishes are gathered from other areas of the house if eating is allowed outside the kitchen.

- If the dishwasher is ready to be loaded, you can supervise while everyone places their own dishes in the dishwasher. Show them that plates go on the bottom, cups on the top, and silverware in the basket for that purpose.

- Water pressure is normally stronger on the bottom rack so place the dirtiest dishes there. This will be your pots and pans so make sure the inside faces the center of your dishwasher where the water will come from. You also may choose to wash your pot and pans by hand, creating more space in your dishwasher for other dishes.

- Separate silverware into the pockets in the rack, but make sure they are not clumped together too closely, or the water stream will not be able to access them.

- Try pouring white vinegar in the compartment for rinse agents. It is cheaper and should work just as well as other rinse agents. It will keep your dishes extra shiny.

- When unloading the dishwasher, begin with the dishes from the bottom rack. This will prevent any standing water remaining on dishes from the top rack from spilling down onto your clean dishes.

Determine where eating is allowed in the home

Another thing you need to decide is exactly where you will allow eating to take place in your home. This may depend on the age of your children, but what you decide will also determine how much clutter you have around the house. If you allow eating in the bedrooms, there will be crumbs and trash to contend with. If you allow eating in your family room, then all dishes need to be returned to the kitchen when snack time is over. Some snacks are more portable and less messy than others. Grapes or apples may not be a problem, but a peanut butter and jelly sandwich is a different story.

Ask yourself these questions to outline your own rules:

- Will you allow dishes to be taken outside to the deck, patio, or yard area?

- Will you allow eating in the car? If so, can your dishes be taken to the car as well?

- If you do allow eating outside of the kitchen or dining area, who will be responsible for bringing those items back to the kitchen?

- If you do not want food in other areas of the home, could you bring out a sheet or towel to be used for special movie nights and popcorn?

You can consider allowing this on a trial basis, but if the rules are broken, the privilege of eating outside the kitchen is revoked. Or, you may wish to allow it during special occasions. Either way, you must guard against sticky cups with leftover juice being abandoned in the car, bedroom, or yard because ants are sure to find them no matter where they are left behind.

The next chapter will examine how to use your attic or basement area for additional storage for your belongings, outlining what you should avoid when using these spaces.

Chapter 10

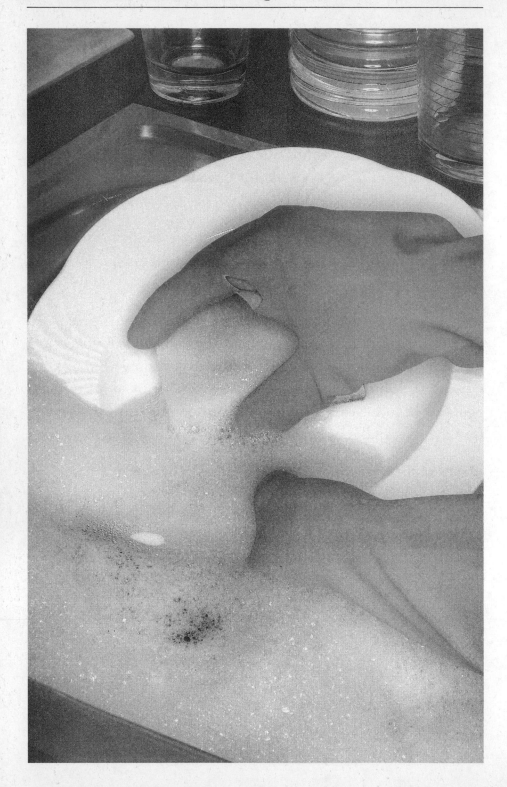

Attacking Your Attic, Basement, or Garage

In order to keep your home uncluttered and functional, you must take advantage of any additional storage space provided by an attic, basement, or garage. Because few homes offer the luxury of having all three of these options, you must seize the space you have and make it work for you and your family.

Your garage should be reserved for your vehicle or vehicles. It protects your vehicle from the elements, the heat, and from the dangers of theft or vandalism. But, if your home has neither an attic nor basement, you must develop a plan of action that does not sacrifice the space meant for your vehicles. With the right storage systems, you can find a way to end up with a garage that does not embarrass you as soon as the doors open.

With your attic or basement, it is important to know how to properly set these spaces up so they will protect your items that are stored there. Just as with the earlier topic of rented storage units mentioned in Chapter 2, do not store your leftover items just because you have not figured out what to do with them. Every item that takes up space in your home, even in your attic or basement, must be there for a reason, must have a designated home, and must earn the right to stay there. The less these areas are cluttered with unwanted junk, the easier they will be to maintain.

Before you decide how to best take advantage of these spaces, examine how to keep unwanted pests out of all areas of your home.

Critter-proofing all areas of your home

Regardless of where you choose to store your belongings, you need to make certain your home is protected from unwelcome critters of all shapes and sizes that seek to damage and feast on your treasures. The popular magazine *The Family Handyman* offers these tips and methods for preventing critter invasions in your home in the following article, found at their website: **www.familyhandyman.com/DIY-Projects/Outdoor-Projects/Yard/Pests/how-to-keep-pests-out-of-your-house/Step-By-Step**.

To critter-proof your home as completely as possible, follow the steps listed below.

1. Find and eliminate any access points for pests into your home.

   • Check for danger spots by going into your attic or basement on a sunny day. Check for outdoor light that filters through under doors, around windows, or through the ceiling or walls.

   • Add a chimney cap to cover your chimney.

- Check for worn out weather stripping underneath your doors, especially a garage door. Torn window screens are also an easy access point for critters.

- Trim any trees and bushes away from the roof or windows of your home. They provide the easiest access to your roof areas.

- Seal any gaps you find with polyurethane caulking. Though it is messy to install, it remains sticky for long-term protection.

2. Be aware of moisture problems.

   - Seal any leaks around pipes beside the house or pipes underneath the house. Check under the sinks as well.

   - Rake your mulch often so it will absorb moisture better. When reapplying mulch, keep the depth between 2 to 3 inches so it can continue to absorb moisture.

   - Make sure all drainage spouts that drain water from your roof and gutters are unblocked and the water is channeled away from your house at a slope so it will not back up.

   - Get a dehumidifier for your basement or garage area to use as needed. By keeping your humidity levels below 40 percent, spiders and other pests will seek shelter elsewhere because they prefer moist environments.

3. Get rid of clutter.

   - Anything that covers your floors in your attic, garage, or basement invites darkness, moisture, and a perfect haven for unwanted pests.

- Avoid using cardboard boxes because they hold moisture. Use plastic tubs instead.

- Store any tubs on shelves against the wall so the floor is clear, and any signs of an invasion of pests will be easily recognized.

- Be aware of any liquid product leakage, such as cleaning supplies in these areas. Wipe down cabinets often, and make sure all enclosed dark areas are completely dry.

- Do not store brown paper grocery bags in a stack underneath the sink because they draw bugs to them. If you must keep them for future use, place them in a sealed, airtight container.

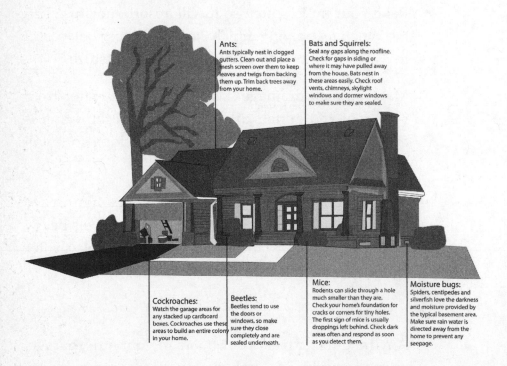

Ants:
Ants typically nest in clogged gutters. Clean out and place a mesh screen over them to keep leaves and twigs from backing them up. Trim back trees away from your home.

Bats and Squirrels:
Seal any gaps along the roofline. Check for gaps in siding or where it may have pulled away from the house. Bats nest in these areas easily. Check roof vents, chimneys, skylight windows and dormer windows to make sure they are sealed.

Cockroaches:
Watch the garage areas for any stacked up cardboard boxes. Cockroaches use these areas to build an entire colony in your home.

Beetles:
Beetles tend to use the doors or windows, so make sure they close completely and are sealed underneath.

Mice:
Rodents can slide through a hole much smaller than they are. Check your home's foundation for cracks or corners for tiny holes. The first sign of mice is usually droppings left behind. Check dark areas often and respond as soon as you detect them.

Moisture bugs:
Spiders, centipedes and silverfish love the darkness and moisture provided by the typical basement area. Make sure rain water is directed away from the home to prevent any seepage.

Up or Down?

When deciding where to store your items, you must first understand the limitations of each area and learn what to do to care for your belongings.

Using your attic space

Your attic can be the perfect place to store items long term as long as you follow the proper techniques. Higher temperatures will always be a factor in attic areas so do not store the following in your attic:

- Electronics
- Photos or film
- Candles
- Delicate fabrics
- Camcorder tapes or VCR videos

However, here are a few tips for proper storage in your attic space:

- Clean it thoroughly. Keep in mind that any signs of pests draw more pests so vacuum, sweep, dust, and air out your attic area often.

- To remove odors, purchase some small activated charcoal discs or loose granules from your pet store near the fish supply equipment. These work great in enclosed areas to neutralize unpleasant odors.

- If your attic has any windows, make sure there is a screen in place and open them often, turning on a fan to pull in the outside air.

- Choose carefully what you store. Items you do not want now will most likely remain unwanted in the future. Unless it is something of great sentimental value that can withstand the heat of the attic, let your excess items go.

- Store items off the floor and around the perimeter of the attic. Do not block air vents or exposed insulation.

- Store items in airtight containers, see-through if possible. Label them on the side where they can easily be read. Rather than writing on the tub itself, place a sticker label or number on it, and keep a list. Many times, tubs are reused and mislabeled because they still show what used to be stored in them.

- Group like items together. Holiday items go in one area, and clothing goes into another area. Keep a clear walkway so items are easily accessible and you do not have to move one stack to get to another.

- Create storage space by hanging bars between rafters or installing bookshelves for books. Boxes of books will rarely be used because no one can find what they are looking for.

- If you store furniture, make sure you only store furniture that will be used again by someone in the near future. Do not keep it just in case. Cover with old sheets or wrap in plastic to protect those valuable pieces.

- Sketch a quick drawing or chart of your attic layout, and post on the door with the date. Label exactly where to find your particular items.

What stores well in the basement

To best determine what can safely be stored in your basement areas, it is important to examine the parameters of using this space. Basements are known for being dark, musty, and perfect spots for mold and mildew to grow so make sure any problems with moisture are resolved from the start. Many times, drainage issues outside the house cause these problems from standing water. For incidental problems with moisture, purchase a dehumidifier or use cat litter wrapped in old socks to absorb the moisture.

Again, before looking at what stores well in basement areas, you must first identify what does not. Do not store the following items in your basement if there is any sign of dampness or a musty smell:

- Bedding, such as pillows, comforters, or sheets, unless they are stored in a moisture-proof container
- Clothing
- Photos or film
- Any wood items
- Baseball card collections
- Any valuable paper records
- Records or CDs
- Food or perishable items
- Musical instruments
- Anything in cardboard boxes because they are not airtight and will draw bugs to them

There are still many items that can be stored easily in your basement space. This space is cooler year-round, and with the right preparation, you can still take advantage of your basement space. Consider the following suggestions for the best use of this space:

- Remember to keep the floor as clear as possible so you quickly recognize any signs of trouble, such as moisture problems or unwelcome pests. Use shelves against the walls and keep a clear pathway.

- Cleaning products store well in the basement; just make sure to keep them out of the reach of children.

- Store your out-of-season lawn or patio furniture in this space.

- Dishes, glass vases, and canning equipment keep well in the basement; just make sure they are safely wrapped and cannot be easily knocked off shelves by children.

- To store camping, fishing, and hunting equipment, spray the dirt off before storing and allow to dry completely.

- The basement makes a great home for tools and toolboxes. Just keep them off the floor to prevent rusting.

As with the attic space, keep items in stackable, see-through containers. Label each one, and chart out where everything is kept. Get rid of any item you know will not be used within the next year.

The Purpose of Your Garage

According to Garage Envy, a garage renovation company located in Los Angeles, there are 65 million garages in the United States, many of which are used as oversized junk drawers.

For this reason, determining a mission statement for every room in your home, as mentioned in Chapter 3, is vitally important for your garage. In its current state, your garage may serve as the home to several items that may or may not belong in the garage. There are some neighborhood associations that impose rules that require all cars to be housed in the garage, with no parking allowed on the curb in front of the home. If this is the case, you have no choice but to create space for your vehicles within your garage.

If you do not make a plan in advance, there will be no room left for your car. Your garage may also be the dumping ground for the uncluttering you have done in other areas of the home. Do not use it as a holding area for things you have not decided what to do with. If you cannot decide what to do with an item, you probably need to get rid of it.

How a garage saves time and money

The following benefits may be just what you need to motivate you to unclutter your garage enough to use it for its original purpose, which is to store your vehicles.

1. Your car insurance rates might decrease.

2. It shields your car from the elements.

3. It saves you time in cold temperatures because you do not have to scrape your windshield, and your car will warm up much sooner.

4. It saves you money in car repairs from incidental dents and scratches.

5. It protects your car from vandalism or theft.

Now that you have good reason to create space for your vehicles inside your garage, there should still be plenty of room for storing other large items, if you choose the right system.

Garage storage systems

No longer a neglected part of the home, garages are the No. 1 area that homeowners have spent money trying to improve in recent years. In order to take advantage of this additional space, while still allowing room for your vehicles, look into these products created specifically for garages:

- Peg board wall systems to hang tools and other objects

- Versatile shelving installed into the wall for stability

- Overhead shelving to take advantage of the tall ceiling space the garage offers

- Specific hanging kits for sporting goods like golf or ski equipment and bikes

- Tool cabinets designed especially for large tool collections

- Locked, freestanding cabinets to keep dangerous items out of the reach of children and pets

- Storage cabinets at eye level

- Corner bins or stands designed for sporting goods or yard tools

The number of products to assist with garage organization is endless. Borrow ideas from the experts, and just as with the inside of your home, designate a space for everything.

Eight Ways to Reclaim Your Car Space

According to the American Community Survey, people spend an average of 100 hours a year commuting to work, which does not take into consideration carpools, running errands, or driving your kids around town to their various sports practices and dance classes. For this reason, vehicles become almost a "home on wheels" for families. The condition of your vehicle is just as important as that of your home. In order to best take advantage of the time you and your family spend in transit, make an effort to reorganize and stock your vehicle so you have what you need without junking up your mobile space.

You need the following items as you begin this process of reorganizing your car.

- An expandable file folder the size of an mailing envelope to fit in your glove box

- Zippered pouch, as used in school notebooks

- A steno notepad

- A container of baby wipes

- A laundry basket or crate to keep in the trunk to hold wandering items or grocery bags

- A small flashlight

- An unused small pizza box to hold markers and coloring books for the kids

It is best to start with a completely clean vehicle, wiping clean the fingerprints and smudges inside the windows and any leftover stickiness around your cup holders. Vacuum your car floor, floor mats, and seats, and add an air freshener of your choice. From this point, consider these suggestions to reorganize:

1. Use the file folder to store all registration, maintenance records, and proof of insurance inside your glove box. Remove any outdated papers, such as car insurance documents, and dispose of them properly. Never store your car title in your car, as it is gone with the car if ever stolen.

2. Use a plastic bag to create a quick first aid kit with bandages, tweezers, fingernail clippers, and anti-bacterial ointment. Place it in your glove box if there is room.

3. Though global positioning systems (GPS) are replacing maps, place any maps or abbreviated version of the Yellow Pages in the door pocket of your passenger's door.

4. Store the baby wipes in your center console, making sure you can reach them while driving. These come in handy for quick cleanups, especially sticky spills or splashes.

5. Create a permanent way to handle trash. Even if you hang a plastic grocery bag over a back seat door handle, make sure everyone uses it. Throw it away every time you refill on gas, and replace with a new one. Keep your supply of bags rolled neatly in your side door pocket.

6. To keep electronic cords and various car chargers from getting tangled, wrap each one around an empty toilet paper roll and stash the ends inside. Line these up inside your center console, and they should be easily accessible when needed.

7. Keep a laundry basket or plastic milk crate in your trunk area for loose items and for preventing groceries from

scattering. If the basket slides around too much, place an old towel underneath.

8. Take in what you bring out, and make sure your family does the same. Use idle time at gas pumps to throw away trash and put things back where they belong. If you leave the inside of your vehicle in good shape each night, your mornings will be off to a better start as well.

In the next section, you will learn to properly store and dispose of those materials that are considered hazardous or poisonous.

Tip #10

O p p r e s s t h e M e s s

What is Household Hazardous Waste?

It is no longer legal, though consequences vary by community, to dispose of the following items by pouring them down the drain, in the ground, or even placing them in regular trash receptacles. At this point, all efforts are being placed on educating communities by offering specific drop-off dates and locations. The items considered to be "hazardous" might surprise you.

- Adhesives (liquid)
- Bleach
- Brake fluid
- Computer systems
- Cooking grease
- Detergent
- Flea collars
- Insect repellent
- Lighter fluid
- Mothballs
- Oven cleaner
- Paint thinner
- Pool chemicals
- Rat and mouse poison
- Transmission fluid

Storing flammable or poisonous chemicals

Many of the products already in your home are considered poisonous or flammable and must be strategically placed out of reach of children. There are more than 2.5 million cases of accidental poisonings being reported each year at the 61 Poison Control Centers in the United States. Of those, more than half involve children younger than 6 with products found in and around the home. These hazardous products can include everything from cleaning supplies, adhesives, arts and crafts materials, automotive fluids, paints, and pesticides. For this reason, it is vitally important to understand how best to store dangerous chemicals.

Use the following guidelines to protect your family from such hazards:

- Leave products in their original containers, clearly identifying the contents.

- Write the date of purchase with a permanent marker and circle or rewrite the expiration date.

- Do not store any hazardous item in a container previously used for food. Small children recognize containers long before they can read.

- Check storage instructions to determine the best temperature for your items. If your garage is extremely hot or cold during seasonal changes, it may destroy the effectiveness of your chemicals. Even worse, the magnified heat could inflame any flammable items.

- Use alternative natural products, or make your own cleaning products to increase the safety in your home.

It is also important to understand how to properly dispose of such products. The rules have changed drastically regarding chemicals and poisonous products, also known as hazardous waste.

Proper Disposal of Household Hazardous Waste

It is estimated that Americans generate more than 1.6 million tons of hazardous waste per year. For this reason, it is important to realize that based on the Resource Conservation and Recovery Act, enacted in 1976, the Environmental Protection Agency now governs all hazardous waste from start to finish, making it illegal to dispose of hazardous items without following their specific guidelines. For example, you are no longer allowed to pour certain substances down the drain or even onto the ground, such as paint, varnish, motor oil, antifreeze, shoe polish, and other chemicals that may infiltrate the water systems. Ink cartridges, batteries, and electronic waste offer dangers as well. At the very least, you must educate yourself on what is now considered hazardous waste. To find the guidelines for your particular community, check with your local public works agency. The Metro Nashville Public Works agency provides a great educational brochure on this topic, regardless of which community you might live in, at **www.nashville.gov/Recycle/pdfs/HHWBrochure.pdf**.

Electronic waste, also known as e-waste, refers to old items like monitors, televisions, VCRs, stereos, fax machines, copiers, and even ink cartridges. There are contaminants built within these products that make them dangerous for the environment or for workers who are not prepared to handle them properly. A great resource for information on recycling and how to properly dispose of such items is the Staples® Soul program. They offer rewards for the donations of ink cartridges but charge a $10 handling and shipping fee to take any personal electronics, such as computers, televisions, monitors, or hardware systems off of your hands. For additional information on this program, visit their website at **www.staples.com/sbd/content/about/soul/recycling.html**.

Next, this book will look at ways to recycle all kinds of items from the home. Recycling can incorporate any action that keeps your belongings and even your trash from ending up in the local landfill. Recycling can mean that you donate unused belongings to those who can benefit further from them, and it can mean that you use items in your home to create new items. When considering whether to recycle, think of giving your items a new purpose rather than immediately disposing of them.

Chapter 11

New to the
Recycling Movement

A ccording to the popular website Earth911®, found at http://earth911.com, recycling is the process of taking a product at the end of its useful life and using all or part of it to make another product. The recycling process requires advanced planning, time, and effort, but the end result is that it saves you money, conserves energy, and protects the resources available. Children are being taught about this at school and through current educational programs so it is important for you to understand the ramifications of your choices as well. You might consider placing your older children in charge of the recycling practices in your own home. Allow them to be the experts and share what they learn. For an immediate education on the topic of recycling, visit the "Recyclopedia" at the Earth 911 website at http://earth911.com/recycling/.

Making Treasures
Out of Your Leftovers

America is known as the land of plenty, and having too much stuff is often the result. The items that go unused in your home may truly be valuable to someone else. Your children will learn the act of giving on a regular basis by watching your actions. If you establish an annual process of culling out unused items in your home to give to people who need them, it will not only cut down on your clutter, but it also will instill in your children a deep awareness to the needs of others. If a stack of blankets falls out every time the linen closet door opens, consider donating some of them to someone in need. If your children have more T-shirts than they could possibly wear in a month, have them go through the shirts and give half of them to a local shelter.

As you unclutter your home, consider some of the following ideas as ways to get rid of your excess while helping those in need.

Out-of-the-Box Donations

If you seek a regular way to make a difference, consider donating the following items to these organizations Though it may create a bit more work to divide and distribute these items, it may develop into an ongoing project for your family. These unique, nonprofit organizations are always in need of the exact items you are placing in your giveaway boxes.

- **Blankets and quilts** — Project Linus has chapters in all states and accepts donations of new, handmade, or used blankets to be distributed to children in hospitals or shelters. For more information, check their website at **www. projectlinus.org/help.html**.

- **Books** — There are libraries at churches, day care centers, hospitals, nursing homes, schools, and orphanages that always need children's books. But, to donate books on the adult reader level, consider donating soft cover books to Prison Book Program in your area. For a list of charities such as this that accept donations, check their website at **www.prisonbookprogram.org/otherprograms.php**. Another option for books and DVDs is to donate to the Books for Soldiers program. Though it requires an application to be notarized in advance, it opens the line of communication so you can donate many other items to aid in the comfort of our soldiers serving abroad. For additional information on this program, visit **http://booksforsoldiers.com.**

- **Clothing, (primarily business attire)** — There are various programs around the country that support training of people to re-enter the work force after an extended period of joblessness for various reasons. In order for this to take place, they need the proper clothing. For women's clothing, consider the Dress for Success® program at **www.dressforsuccess.org**. For men's clothing, try the Career Gear program at **http://careergear.org**.

- **DVDs** — A program called Kidflicks seeks to establish video libraries in children's hospitals around the country. They no longer accept any in VHS format, but as your children outgrow their DVD collection, this could be a great way to recycle them. Check their donation instructions at **www.kidflicks.org**.

- **Electronics** — According to the Environmental Protection Agency, only 18 percent of the 2.25 million tons of unwanted electronic equipment is recycled, leaving the rest to unnecessarily fill our landfills each year. Donate your unneeded electronics as quickly as possible because of the value of electronics declines quickly. Clear your personal information off before donating, but know that if they are less than 5 years old, your used computers, monitors, gaming systems, or televisions can be put to great use. To save on shipping costs, call your local school system or a private school to see if they accept donations or take to any Goodwill location. Goodwill and Dell have collaborated to form a partnership that uses electronic items to serve the mission of Goodwill. For participating locations, check their website at **http://reconnectpartnership.com/locations.php**.

- **Eyeglasses and hearing aids** — New Eyes for the Needy is a great program for recycling both hearing aids and prescription eyeglasses. You can organize a glasses drive at your local church or school, and send donations to their home office in New Jersey. From there, they are sent around the world as needed. For additional information, see their website at **http://neweyesfortheneedy.com/impact/shipping.html**.

- **Sporting equipment** — Everything including old soccer balls, footballs, stopwatches, and uniforms is distributed to underprivileged kids in programs around the country and other countries through the Sports Gift program. Housed in California, all donations are tax deductible, and your family may even receive a photo of children playing with some of your donated gear. For additional information, including tips on shipping and a printable address label, visit **http://sportsgift.org**.

Next, this book will look at some other creative ways to pass along items your family may not need but someone else may want.

Charities

Try not to place too much emphasis on what charity to choose or spread yourself too thin trying to deliver items all over town to many different organizations. Do your own research, and set up a regular process for how, when, and where to donate. Many charities pick up everything for you, right off your front porch, and leave you a receipt along with a sense of pride and a less cluttered home.

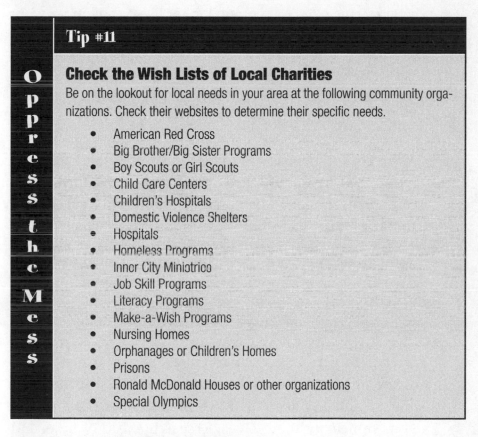

Tip #11

O p p r e s s t h e M e s s

Check the Wish Lists of Local Charities

Be on the lookout for local needs in your area at the following community organizations. Check their websites to determine their specific needs.

- American Red Cross
- Big Brother/Big Sister Programs
- Boy Scouts or Girl Scouts
- Child Care Centers
- Children's Hospitals
- Domestic Violence Shelters
- Hospitals
- Homeless Programs
- Inner City Ministries
- Job Skill Programs
- Literacy Programs
- Make-a-Wish Programs
- Nursing Homes
- Orphanages or Children's Homes
- Prisons
- Ronald McDonald Houses or other organizations
- Special Olympics

Coat and clothing drives

Many churches host annual coat collections, donating winter gear they collect to needy families in their area, while also providing information on how those families can seek further assistance for their future physical and emotional needs.

Clothing drives may be more difficult to find but are a great way to get rid of your unused clothing. For example, after the massive earthquakes in Haiti and Chile in 2010, there were clothing drives across America that only requested T-shirts of all sizes that were quickly shipped to charities already working on the ground in these areas so they could be distributed to the earthquake victims.

Giving away your car

If you have a vehicle or boat you no longer use or no longer want to invest money repairing, consider donating it to charity. The advantage is that even if the vehicle is no longer running, it can be picked up at the expense of the charity, saving you towing or transportation costs. Be aware of the following guidelines to make sure you get the most value for your donation:

- Make sure to choose your charity carefully and that it is recognized by the IRS as a 501(c)(3) organization so you can properly deduct the donation on your taxes. Look for those that offer a fair market value for your vehicle.

- You will need to prove the value of the vehicle with a receipt from your chosen charity to use when filing your taxes. Keep a copy of the car title before signing it over to them as well.

- If you truly wish for a particular charity to benefit, be aware of organizations that serve as the middle man and end up actually keeping 50 to 90 percent of the value of your vehicle for themselves. Research ahead of time, and check them through the Better Business Bureau.

- Seek charities that keep their donations in your local area. Many will fix up cars and resell them to low-income families who need the transportation in order to find a job. Doing this ensures your donation makes a difference in your own community.

- Notify your insurance agency that the car no longer needs to be insured.

Give your stuff away day

Instituting a day where everyone in a community places unneeded items on their curbs has recently become popular. Also known as Curb Day, passers-by can go from house to house and take whatever items they need. It is important to remove your items at the end of the day. Though you do not get the tax advantage from this type of giveaway, it does prevent your larger items from ending up in a landfill and might just help a nearby family in need. For additional information, visit **http://giveyourstuffaway.com**.

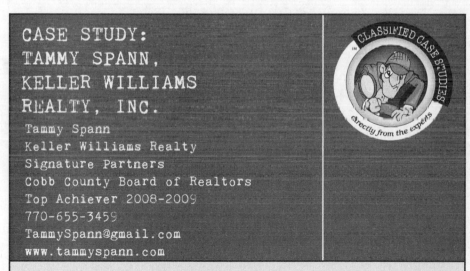

CASE STUDY:
TAMMY SPANN,
KELLER WILLIAMS
REALTY, INC.

Tammy Spann
Keller Williams Realty
Signature Partners
Cobb County Board of Realtors
Top Achiever 2008-2009
770-655-3459
TammySpann@gmail.com
www.tammyspann.com

Tammy Spann is a Realtor serving the North Atlanta and West Cobb areas of Georgia. Recognized by the Cobb Board of Realtors as a Top Achiever for 2008 and 2009, she recently participated in the National Association of Realtor's Green Designation Team, which identifies her as an expert in the latest trends for going green in the home.

Through her exposure to countless homes she has also become an expert on the topic of de-cluttering and organizing a home in a way that best serves the homeowner, as well as their guests. Spann offers many suggestions to her clients on how to recycle without increasing the clutter in the home, as well as ways to keep the family involved. Recycling, just as with de-cluttering, requires forethought, commitment, and most of all, an outlined plan of action.

The practice of recycling mirrors the thought process behind efforts to unclutter as well. Everything has value, and if it is not being used in your home, take it somewhere it can be used. Do not waste time, energy, or space on items you do not need.

To help take this idea to a new level in your own home, Spann offers the following tips that not only conserve energy and protect the environment but that will also cut down on the clutter in your home by decreasing the amount of trash your family produces and the number of new products they bring inside the home:

Use only cloth napkins. Avoid using paper or plastic products if possible.

Download books or read newspapers online to save a tree, as well as money, and significantly cut down on the clutter in the home.

Buy a water bottle for each person in family to reuse, labeling it with the name of each family member.

Get plastic trash cans and label them to separate specific goods. Line each with a trash bag, and fill with cans, glass, and white paper or cardboard. Make a weekly trip to drop off the recyclables, and allow the kids to turn them in to the drop-off center.

Set thermostats to 78 in summer and 68 in winter.

The best advice she has to offer for families is to plant a vegetable garden — it gets everyone involved, is good for the environment, decreases trips to the grocery store, is cheaper than buying your produce, and brings a sense of pride for the entire family when they see and taste the "fruits" of their labor.

Using color-coded recycling bins makes it easy for everyone in the family to recycle. Recycling also helps reduce your household trash and keeps reusable items out of landfills.

Chapter 12

Transforming
Trash into Cash

There are various ways to take what you consider junk and transform it into cash. For someone in the process of uncluttering the home, you have a dual purpose in doing this: to clear your home of unused items and to make a profit, if possible. There are many companies that, for a small fee, can assist with this, handling the advertising and selling process for you. This chapter will examine your options so you can choose which company best meets your needs.

Tip #12

Oppress the Mess

Merchandise Buyback Programs

Before trashing your broken appliances, check to see if there is some sort of trade-in or buyback offer to take that item off your hands and help you replace it with a new one. Here are a few programs currently available, and though they may be in place for a limited time, they provide examples as to what is available if you are willing to search:

- Similar to the "Cash for Clunkers" program, the federal government sponsored a program offering cash rebates for older appliances that are turned in and replaced with energy efficient models. Energy Star-qualified appliances that are eligible for these rebates include air conditioners, both window units and central units, boilers, washing machines, heat pumps and furnaces, dishwashers, water heaters, and refrigerators or freezers.

- Gold and silver buyback programs for jewelry have increased across the nation, both online and in stores. If you are nervous about mailing in your jewelry before receiving any payment, take them to a company that pays on the spot, and check each business through the Better Business Bureau before deciding to do business with them.

- Many police departments offer a gun trade-in program, offering money to take guns off the streets.

- Toys"R"Us has a buyback program for old video games, providing store credit in exchange for them. The games are actually sold to a third-party dealer that refurbishes them and resells them, but it is a great way to update your collection.

- iResQ is an online company that buys back, at a fairly good price, broken iPods, iPads, iPhones, and Macbooks. They also repair these products and sell refurbished items. For additional information, visit **www.iresq.com**.

Identifying the Different Types of Consignment or Resale Options

The term "consignment" refers to turning over something to be sold on your behalf. It is a way to resell used goods, and there are many methods of doing this. Consignment shops are known for providing items that are in better condition than the typical thrift store, but their prices are higher as well.

Consignment shops are categorized into specialty stores, featuring women's clothing in one, children's items in another, and furniture in another. They are particular about what they accept, require that items are cleaned and repaired in advance, and might keep as much as 50 percent of the sales price of your items. Many stores come and go quickly so choose one that has been in business for a long time and that is in a good location for customer traffic. Most shops do not provide payment for your items until they are sold, and they pay their sellers on a quarterly or semiannual basis.

There are some trusted national consignment chains that practice the same operating procedures, regardless of their home city. Though these stores may keep a greater portion of the profits, the level of professionalism and trust is higher than that of an individually owned store. Here are a few of the national stores, and what they feature:

- **Plato's Closet®** — This retail store features name brand clothing for teens and 20-somethings. For locations, visit **www.platoscloset.com**.

- **Once Upon a Child®** — This store boasts the largest chain of "kid's stuff with previous experience." For locations, see **www.onceuponachild.com**.

- **Children's Orchard®** — This store pays cash for high-quality children's clothing and furniture, now offering items online as well at **www.childrensorchard.com**.

- **Buffalo Exchange®** — This store provides vintage women's clothing. For locations, visit their website at **www.buffalo exchange.com**.

- **Restore ReSale Outlet** — This is actually a part of the Habitat for Humanity Program®, offering building materials, furniture, fixtures, and home accessories to raise money to build their homes. It also offers online sales. For additional information, visit **www.habitat.org/env/restores.aspx**.

- **Play it Again Sports®** — This sports store pays cash for used sporting goods in good condition. For more information, see **www.playitagainsports.com**.

EBay stores as a way to sell items

EBay proves to be a way to make money from your own hidden treasures. With so many users, the chances are great that someone out there is desperately looking for the very item that is taking up space in your garage, attic, or basement.

If you only have a few items for sale, rather than taking the time to learn the rules, set up an account, photograph your items, choose your prices and a timeline to accept bids on those items, you might benefit from many stores that sell on eBay that do all the work for you. Selling everything from electronics to video games, home goods to furniture, and musical equipment to sporting goods, they keep a small percentage of any sales. But, because they offer the quickest way to get your hand-me-downs into the hands of an actual buyer, it just may be worth it to you. Some stores even offer to pick up your items for free. Below is a list of a few of these national chain stores with their website information:

1. Pickup 2 Sell — **www.pickup2sell.com/index.htm**
2. I Sold It® on eBay — **http://877isoldit.com/**
3. Snappy Auctions™ — **www.snappyauctions.com/index. php**

The next section will look at the daunting task of hosting your own sale.

Selling Everything but the Yard

Besides consignment and Internet sales, another way to make money from your excess stuff is to host your own garage or yard sale. This requires a great amount of effort, planning ahead, and time. Customers often ask for a lower price than what you have listed. Be ready to bargain, and aim low on your expectations of profit. Ask yourself if it is worth the effort if you make less than $100 before making the commitment to go through with your sale. Many factors contribute to or hinder the success

Selling items through online auctions and websites is a great way to get rid of your unused items, as well as earn additional income.

of a sale, and rarely does it have to do with the quality of items offered there. Location, weather, time of year, and the personal needs of your customers will determine how many people show up and how much they spend. You might have a perfectly good piano priced at $100, but if none of your customers need a piano, it will not sell.

As a general rule, the following items sell well at moving, yard, or garage sales.

- Antique furniture
- Appliances in working order
- Area rugs
- Audio/visual equipment, such as cameras and stereos
- Auto accessories like floor mats, seat and steering wheel covers
- Baby furniture and equipment
- Bikes and other riding toys
- Board and party games, if all the pieces are in place
- Books
- Camping equipment
- CDs or DVDs
- Cookware
- Furniture
- Kitchen items
- Musical instruments
- Patio furniture
- Photography equipment
- Plants
- Sporting goods
- Tools
- Toys

Make sure everything works, or clearly state any problems with your items, such as missing pieces from a set, a broken knob on a stereo, or a lamp that does not work. With the right price combined with an honest approach, you might be able to sell items that are slightly damaged. To assist in the success of your sale, try the suggestions from the following checklist.

Garage Sale Checklist

Before making the commitment to hold a sale, ask yourself the following questions:

- Do you and your family have time to organize a garage sale?
- Would you buy the items you have to offer?
- Are your items in good condition?
- Is your home's location easy to access for a successful garage sale?
- Will you have people available to help on the actual day of the sale?
- Can you convince others in your community to hold a sale on the same day?

Once you have made the commitment, choose a date, and get organized doing the following:

- Save grocery bags and boxes for your customers to use to carry out their purchases.
- Borrow as many tables as possible for your displays.
- Get a hanging rack on wheels if you plan to sell clothes and gather extra hangers.
- Make an inventory list of everything you plan to sell. Arrange by category.
- Schedule volunteers to help on the day of the sale.
- Make a plan for pets on that day to keep them safe from the extra traffic and to keep your customers safe from your pets.
- Borrow cash boxes or use fanny packs to store money and make change for customers. Get a calculator, pens, and a receipt book for your checkout station.
- Temporarily remove any items from your garage that will not be for sale.
- If you hold a sale outside, make a plan for bad weather. Hang a canopy or clear out space to move indoors if needed.

Advertise in advance, using as many of these methods as possible:

- Invite your friends using Facebook®, Twitter®, or e-mail. Send a reminder the day before.
- Make signs showing the date, address, and times, and hang in high-traffic areas.
- Place signs on community bulletin boards in neighborhood stores.
- On the day of the sale, place signs with arrows directing them to your home. Add a balloon to each sign to draw attention.

Clearly price all items in the following manner:

- Calculate what your profits would be if you sold everything, and then estimate about 30 percent of that total.
- Use a consistent pricing method, color-coding by specific stickers. All orange tags are $1, green tags are $5, blue tags are $10, etc.
- Never write a price directly on an item. Use stickers instead.
- Charge about 20 percent of the original cost of an item if it is in good condition.
- Price items as a set, such as a set of dishes, but be ready to separate if requested. Someone may be interested in a platter without taking your entire set of dishes.
- If you have a lot of a particular item, price them as a group, such as four books for $1, allowing visitors to pick what they want.
- If you are holding a joint sale with other families, separate items by different colored stickers and determine a plan to keep up with that at the checkout. Use separate cash boxes or keep a list. Customers will buy items from all families and will want to pay at one time.
- Be prepared to reduce your prices when a customer asks. Bartering is a part of the process.
- Make a plan to lower prices at a certain time of the day to get rid of as many items as possible. This, along with the fact that customers will frequently negotiate a lower price, makes it almost impossible to predict exactly how much you might make off a sale.
- Decide if you are willing to accept checks. People generally do not carry much cash with them so for higher-priced items, they may offer to pay by check. But, if the check bounces, you are stuck with the loss. Because most homeowners have no way to process credit card transactions, you will need to hold an item while someone gets cash or not allow them to pick up the item until the check has cleared. Either way, post your policy clearly.

Display all items as if in a real store — by category, size, and color:

- Place similar items together on a table, bin, or a shelf.
- Label each category with a sign on the wall or table. For example, place bedding, books, or toys together.
- Wash and hang all clothing. Clothes look much better hung.
- Make all items look and smell appealing. Be sure to clean mirrors, wash dishes, and dust furniture.

- Spread toys out on a piece of carpet on the ground so kids can play with them. Parents will often buy them if they see their children enjoying them.
- Even if you are co-hosting a sale, keep all like items together. Do not sort items by family.
- Keep all electronics together, and run extension cords and power strips to plug everything in and turn them on.
- Use any lamps you have for sale to keep your electronics table well lit.
- Place electronics in a secure location, and keep this area staffed at all times for questions.
- Clean the dust off of all electronics and computer equipment, including monitors.
- Turn volume down on all pieces of equipment so it does not startle your guests when turned on.
- Add fans to blow on your electronics table because it might generate a lot of heat from the equipment.
- Place a "not for sale" sign on any items used for display only, such as power strips and fans.

To manage your sale, ensure a level of safety by doing the following:

- Keep at least two workers present at all times.
- Establish a clear checkout area, and have someone keep an eye on what customers are loading into their vehicles.
- Lock the doors to your residence, and leave someone inside the residence to watch for suspicious activity.
- At all times, keep an eye on small children who come with their parents. The parents might get busy looking for items and temporarily lose sight of their kids. Keep them away from any passing cars.
- Stick to your posted hours of operation because you advertised in advance, but plan to arrive early because your customers will most likely do the same. If you run out of items and have to end early, have someone to explain that to any customers.
- Be aware of any suspicious characters that come by and seem to be asking odd questions about your home. Notify the local police if you ever feel you are in danger for any reason.
- If you receive any large bills, have someone inconspicuously take them inside the house at certain intervals of the day.

Junk removal services that make donations

If you are facing a quick deadline for getting rid of your excess belongings and are to the point of donating any and all items, deciding it is not worth the effort required to advertise and sell your stuff, then find a junk removal service that does all the work for you. Look for companies that take the time to donate or sell any recyclable items so they do not end up in your city dump or landfill. They will charge you to pick up your stuff, usually based on volume rather than the time it takes to load the truck, but it may be worth it to know that at the end of the day, the junk is gone for good. A few of these companies that have collaborations with donation centers in each community are listed below:

1. 1800GotJunk® —**www.1800gotjunk.com** charges by volume rather than by the hour and attempts to donate for resale or recycle as much as possible.

2. Just Junk® — **www.justjunk.com/** donates or recycles up to 60 percent of all items picked up.

3. College Hunks Hauling Junk — **www.1800junkusa. com/** originally started by a group of college guys trying to make a little money on the side; they are now available in various cities across the United States. Not only do they recycle and donate items, but they also contribute to scholarships at local colleges in each community.

The next chapter will examine how to unclutter the space used as an office inside the home.

Chapter 13

Uncluttering
Your Office Space

A home office area can refer to the area of your home used to manage the "business" side of running a family. It may be a desk area on wheels in the corner of a bedroom, basement, or family room, or it could be as simple as a hanging wall sorter that holds your bills, stamps, and coupons. You may have a complete room of your home designated to be an office, or you may run a business from your home, which means that your home also serves as your work environment. Regardless of whether you have an actual office to call your own, you still need a way to keep the family paperwork under control.

If you do run a business from your home, it is difficult to separate free time from working hours, and there will be a constant tug of war for your attention. Though many love the freedom of working from home, with no contact from other employees, as in a business environment, your desk may quickly become cluttered and unmanageable simply because you may feel that no one will see it besides yourself.

CASE STUDY:
GAIL GRAY, A FRESH START
PROFESSIONAL ORGANIZING

Gail Gray
A Fresh Start Professional Organizing
2973 Harbor Blvd., #419
Costa Mesa, CA 92626
gail@afreshstartorganizing.net
www.afreshstartorganizing.net

Gail Gray spent the past three years working in the field of professional organization. She excels in finding ways to help a home make sense,

establishing rhyme and reason to storage methods for her clients. Her greatest asset is the fact that she is a busy mother of two and an entrepreneur working from home so she lives the same busy life as her clients. She is a mother who is not naturally organized so like her clients she also has to work at staying organized. Gray knows what it is like to never have enough time, which makes the need for organization and stability amid the chaos even more important.

One of Gray's favorite products that she recommends for her clients is drawer organizers made by Rubbermaid. These create a home for every object in your drawer, and make everything easy to find. She also loves to use open storage containers within cabinets, creating a pullout drawer on each shelf. This keeps items from being knocked over in the back — something she refers to as the "bowling effect." Her preference would be to design all cabinets with pullout shelves so items can be easily retrieved when needed. She uses hooks in all areas of the home to designate a resting spot for items used on a daily basis.

When working with her clients, she recognizes some of the difficulty they have letting go of personal belongings but not for the reasons she expected. "I don't see as much of a struggle to let go of personal memorabilia as the guilt felt by letting go of something that cost a great amount of money," Gray said. "I have to remind my clients that just because you spent money on it does not mean you will recoup your money by leaving it in a cabinet."

Gray regularly encourages them to donate their excess items to the local Goodwill store, which also accepts electronic waste. Many times, people overstress about where to donate their items, but with Goodwill, it is all taken care of at one time and is out of the home for good.

Once the de-cluttering job is complete, to maintain order in the home, Gray teaches a method she refers to as "OHIO," which means Only Handle It Once. "Clutter comes from decisions that have been postponed. Make a decision on what to do with an item the first time you touch it, and your clutter will soon disappear."

"If a family tries to get everything done on the weekend between swim meets and soccer games, it will not get done. If everyone learns to clean up after himself or herself, maintaining the condition of the home is easy."

Home Office Area

Regardless of how you plan to use your home office area, it is important to lay some boundaries to set yourself up for the greatest amount of success. Many companies, including UPS and GM, have clean-desk policies for their employees for the following reasons:

1. It presents the best image when customers visit.

2. It reduces stress for the employees, providing a sense of closure when a task is completed and put away properly.

3. It saves time by making documents easy to find when needed.

4. A tidy desk is a sign of effectiveness.

A clean-desk policy simply states that at the end of each evening, or before expected guests arrive, desks should be as clean as possible. If major corporations recognize the benefits of having a clean desk in order to do the best work, your home will benefit from the same kind of organizational techniques.

To establish your home office, do the following:

This home office is both functional and organized. Everyone in this family uses this office, and as a result, they have set up a filing system on a separate cabinet away from the computer. This ensures no mail will be lost or misplaced. They have also designated a drawer for each person and set up a communal book shelf.

- Define your space. Whatever it is, claim it, and take control of it. Keep all the items you need in that one location. You cannot file items away when completed if your file cabinet is upstairs in another room.

- Keep business files separate from personal files, both in your filing cabinet, as well as on your computer.

- Create a place for everything so piles do not quickly stack up.

- Establish "working hours," and at the end of each workday, leave your desk in good shape for the following day. Print off your to-do list, and have it waiting for you to begin checking things off as soon as you start your next workday.

- Add a bulletin board to keep current projects in view. Think of this as your "big picture." Have a place to jot down ideas for upcoming projects as they come to mind, such as a mouse pad that doubles as a notepad.

- Sort through e-mails daily, and get your inbox set back to zero. Sort an e-mail as soon as you read it, or flag it for further action, and place in a project folder. Never choose to overwhelm yourself by delaying your decisions.

- Avoid the traps of technology. Though everything you need is available 24 hours a day through technology, you are not. Control when you check e-mails, make or accept phone calls, and spend time on social networking sites like Twitter and Facebook.

How to handle incoming mail

A persistent contributor to clutter is the daily stack of incoming mail. One way to manage it is to remove junk mail immediately, saving the rest to process on a weekly basis. Once opened, you must decide at that time what to do with it. Try these tips for managing your family mail system:

1. Establish a drop off point for your mail.

2. When you open it, do so near your recycling bin or filing cabinet so you can put each item in its proper place right away.

3. Place coupons in an organizer you keep with you, either in your car or purse.

4. Buy a paper shredder to destroy personal information, and shred immediately. These remnants can be added to your recycle bin.

5. For any correspondence that requires attention, take to your desk area to complete this task.

Bills

If you do not have a plan in place for paying bills, your money has a way of quickly disappearing before they are paid. The best way to eliminate clutter and take the pressure off of paying bills on time is to set them to draft automatically from your checking account. That way, even if you are out of town or tied up in meetings, these transactions take place on time and without the cost of a stamp to mail in a payment.

Another way to manage the payment of your bills is to set a recurring event on an online calendar, such as Google Calendar® or Microsoft Outlook®. These are easy to use and will send reminders to your e-mail account and can even be forwarded to your cell phone. Once you receive the reminder, you can note the amount, date it was paid, and from which account, saving yourself endless searching later on if any questions arise. For those bills not paid monthly, such as insurance or taxes, set a recurring reminder to set money aside for those larger bills. You never want to be caught off guard by an "unexpected" bill when you had six months or a year to prepare for it.

Designate a place for school papers to be signed each day

With a growing family, it is difficult for parents to keep up with permission slips, notes from the teacher, and important homework assignments. Assign a place for your child to put these items to make sure you see them each night. You can hang wall pockets that you can find at office supply stores just inside the laundry room wall, labeling each one with a particular child's name. This can serve as their "inbox," and it is up to you to check it each night. After signing, you can return the papers to them to be placed in their notebook for school the following day.

Next, this chapter examines ways to share the family computer.

The Home Computer

The family computer will quickly become a hub of activity in your house. Younger children will learn to play games on it in school as early as the kindergarten grade level. Older children need it to type writing assignments or to do research on an assigned topic. In order to prevent the inconvenience of someone accidentally erasing someone else's document, you need to establish some rules to make sure your computer is available for everyone's use when needed.

Consider some of the following guidelines for your home's computer:

- Set a regular schedule for everyone to use the computer based on what time they arrive home from school. For example, Rachel – 3:00 – 3:30 , Hunter – 4:00 – 4:30, dinner time, then each child gets an additional 30 minutes afterward, unless someone needs it specifically for doing homework.

- Reserve it for large blocks of time for those needing to do research projects, and make sure other family members do not hover over them waiting for their turn.

- Set up a log in screen for each family member so they can access their own files and arrange their desktop and documents the way they like.

- Important photos and files should be backed up on a regular basis either with anti-virus software, an online storage program, or external hard drive.

- Establish a location for older students to keep a flash drive to take back and forth to school. Because these are small, easy to lose, and all look the same, carve their initials in the plastic cover using a knife or scissors, and buy them in separate colors so they can tell them apart from the outside, and make sure it is placed in the same place in their backpack every time. You might even add an address label around it in case it gets misplaced.

Tip #13

Oppress the Mess

Uncluttering the Family Computer

In order to keep your shared computer operating as fast as possible for your family, consider these options:

- Refrain from downloading any new programs.
- Remove any unused programs.
- Go into your system tools program and defragment your computer at least once a month. This deletes any unused space on your hard drive, freeing it to function much faster.
- Perform a disk clean-up, also found in your system tools folder. This removes any duplicates or temporary files from your hard drive.
- Schedule these tasks to run automatically on a regular basis, typically when your computer is not in use, such as early in the morning. Make sure your computer is left on when your tasks are scheduled.

Store items on an external source to keep from bogging down your computer, especially if you have many large files such as videos or photographs. Use an external hard drive or flash drive to store them, or store them online with Google documents and keep them available when you log in. There are several other sites that offer free online storage for your documents, such as Huge Drive, found at **www.hugedrive.com/**.

Filing More Than Your Fingernails

Whether you have a home office or not, you must designate a place to store vital family records, preferably a lockable filing cabinet. Ideally, your filing system must be one that is understood by everyone so your family can access important documents if needed. Buy hanging folders with printable tabs. This eliminates the dangers of misfiling something due to poor handwriting.

Create tabs for the following:

- **Appliances** — Keep warranties, receipts for purchase, and operating manuals here.

- **Auto** — Keep title and insurance papers arranged per vehicle in separate folders.

- **Credit/loan records** — Make a folder for all sources of debt and store proof of payment. Make a note when you pay each debt off, and make sure those accounts are closed properly so they do not show on your credit report.

- **Donations and tax deductions** — Keep good records on the value of any and all donations for tax purposes.

- **Family** — Make a tab for each member of the family. Store birth certificates, shot records, school physical forms, and report cards in these folders.

- **Financial records** — Create a separate folder for every banking institution you use.

- **Income tax** — Keep all tax return records from past years here. At the first of each year, designate a large envelope to hold tax records as documentation begins to arrive in the mail.

- **Insurance** — Separate into homeowners, life insurance, health, and auto. Do not keep all insurance papers together.

- **Investments** — Keep all investment records here, even small savings accounts, to make sure none are forgotten.

- **Mortgage or rent** — Keep all documents pertaining to your mortgage or lease here.

- **Pay stubs/employment records** — Keep all employment records and pay stubs for a year at a time.

- **Pet(s)** — Keep veterinary records, registration, and licensing info here.

- **Property tax** — In some states, this is paid twice a year so make sure you have a record of when it is due and proof of payment.

- **Utilities** — Separate tabs for all outgoing monthly bills, including phone, water, cable, electricity, and gas, if applicable.

Going paperless

The best way to keep the size of your files down in your filing cabinets is to go paperless as much as possible. It is a great method of going green and will greatly reduce unwanted paper from stacking up in your house. Follow these ideas to reduce the paper from your life:

- Cancel all paper versions of your bills, and sign up for paperless versions with each company. Your notifications will arrive through e-mail, and you can create a "Paid" e-mail folder so you can move each notification there once it has been paid.

- Eliminate all magazine and newspaper subscriptions, and switch to online versions.

- Only request canceled checks from your bank once a year for tax purposes. Most banks will provide a copy online for you to print as needed.

- Do not overuse your printer. If your children are typing a paper for school, proofread before printing. If a mistake is made, correct and only reprint that page rather than re-printing the entire document.

- Scan important documents, and keep on your external hard drive to preserve older records. This allows you to find with keyword searches and print a copy at a later date if needed.

- Print only when necessary. If you run across an article you like online, bookmark it to review later rather than print-ing and leaving it in a stack.

- Remove yourself from junk mail lists by registering for this free service, offered by Direct Mail™ at **www.directmail. com/directory/mail_preference/**.

The next chapter will examine ways to keep your home neat and tidy, which requires much less effort now that you have less to keep up with.

Chapter 14

Keeping Your Home Running Smoothly

Now that you have removed the excess clutter from the home, you will find that by doing a little at a time, sticking with your routines, and taking advantage of any short-cuts you can find, it is easier than ever to keep it under control. Your neat and tidy spaces will depend on you to keep them that way, and you will need the help of your family to do so.

Set Up a Nightly Routine

Create a nightly routine that does not exhaust you or leave you guessing as to what happens next. You do not want to walk into the kitchen to find a sink full of dirty dishes each morning, which puts you behind schedule before your day even starts. Here are some tips to help keep your newly uncluttered home in great condition.

1. Start your day the night before. Print off a schedule, and make sure everyone is aware of what the next day holds. Line up all backpacks on hooks beside the front door. For school lunches, prepare in advance, placing cold sandwiches in plastic containers in the fridge to be grabbed the next morning.

2. Provide alarm clocks for everyone, and make sure they are set properly each evening. Teach them to wake themselves up on time. It takes everyone working together to get out the door on time so the inaction of one person can slow everyone else down.

3. Complete all of your tasks to ensure your day will be off to a good start. Leave nothing to be done the following day, or you will be behind schedule already.

Tip #14

O p p r e s s   t h e   M e s s

Managing Your Family's Schedule

In order to make sure everyone gets where they need to at just the right time, try these tips:

- Buy a large calendar to write events where everyone can see, even small children. Use a different color for each person in the family.

- Create a computerized calendar, such as Google or Outlook, that family members can share. If you log into a computer each morning for work purposes, set your computer calendar as your home page. Set a task list and quickly add to it as soon as you learn of a new appointment.

- Set your computer calendar to send reminders to your cell phone in advance, even a day early, to make sure any transportation needs are worked out.

- Each evening, review your schedule for the next day.

- Try using Cozi's free online family calendar. It easily color codes each person's schedule, includes a family journal to jot down specific notes from that day (braces off, scored the winning run, etc.), and even has a "to-do" list per family member. Visit **www.cozi.com** for more details.

Maintaining a clean home is done in small increments, taking advantage of any free time. Capture a free 30-minute period while everyone is out of the house to make a quick difference. Take this chance for a quick clean up to lighten the load and the mood for your entire family.

12 Steps to Speed-cleaning While No one Else is Home

There are several tasks you can perform for a quick cleaning fix. Even if you are the only one home, there are several simple tasks you can do to improve your home's appearance. Start with the things that can run without your help. Set a quick pace by racing against your dishwasher or washing machine. By the time the cycles are complete, you will be done as well.

1. Load the dishwasher, and start the cycle.
2. Run a load of laundry at the same time.
3. Spray problem areas in tubs, sinks, and toilets so they can soak.
4. Sprinkle some carpet cleaner powder, and let it sit.
5. Use an empty laundry basket to pick up any out of place items. Place the basket in a central location, and toss things into it as you come across them.
6. Dust furniture from top to bottom before you vacuum or sweep.
7. Wipe down counters in the kitchen and bathrooms with disposable wipes.
8. Sweep kitchen or bathrooms, brushing debris out onto the carpet areas for later vacuuming.

9. Use glass wipes to clean your mirrors.

10. Scrub toilets, sinks, and tubs quickly.

11. Vacuum the carpets. Focus mainly on high-traffic and problem areas.

12. Save the basket of items to be put away, your clean dishes, and laundry for the rest of the family to take care of when they return.

Chores for the children

Another way to help maintain your tidy home, and to motivate your children to continue to help, is to create a chore system for them. They should be expected to help with some tasks simply because they are asked, and because day-to-day family living requires work.

To motivate them without nagging on a regular basis, try establishing a pay scale for chores they do each week. At a rate of 50 cents or a $1 per task, they will come to you seeking additional ways to help. Establish a weekly pay day and have them keep a chart or list of what they have done during the week. Only pay when the work has been completed to satisfaction, and raise the rate for bigger jobs. For example, these are some tasks children can help with each week:

- Folding and delivering the laundry on laundry day
- Gathering the trash and taking to the curb on trash day
- Loading and unloading the dishwasher
- Weeding the garden
- Stripping all the beds

The next section will examine some of the newer products on the market that can assist with your housekeeping duties. Any product that solves a problem and saves time, energy, and money is worth taking a closer look at.

New cleaning gadgets or products that offer shortcuts

Just a few years ago, the Magic Eraser came along to remove all crayon residue across walls. Since then, the latest rage in cleaning has gone to the robots. Some of these new products on the market just might resolve the dirtiest household problems for families.

IRobot® offers the best in electronic cleaning products. For more information on the following gadgets, visit their website at **http://store.irobot.com/home/index.jsp**. With various models available, they range in price from $130 to $700.

- **iRobot Scooba** — This is a floor washing robot that handles your mopping for you.

- **iRobot Roomba** — This is the vacuuming robot with special designs available for homes with hairy pets.

- **iRobot Dirt Dog** — This was designed for vacuuming the garage or warehouse type floors.

Consider these additional electronic cleaning products.

- **Eye Vac Electronic Dust Bin®** — At a price of about $90, first discovered in hair salons, this provides a method of sweeping the floor that does not require bending over. Great for homes with pet hair problems and hardwood floors, you just sweep the debris to the Eye Vac, turn it on, and it sucks the dirt away. It works much better than a dust pan, and even helps to clean the debris off your broom when you are done. For more information, visit **www.comforthouse.com/dustpan.html?feed=ysw**.

- **Dirt Devil Electric Broom®** — A dual-purpose vacuum with the bristles of a broom, this works great on homes with hardwood floors as well and is priced around $70.

For additional information, visit **www.comforthouse. com/dirtdevil4.html**.

- **Scrubbing Bubbles Automatic Shower Cleaner®** — To prevent soap scum and mildew buildup, install an automatic shower cleaner underneath your shower head. Press the button when showering is complete, and the bubbles use the leftover water to clean your tub and shower walls. This product is less than $30. For additional information, visit **www.automaticshowercleaner.com/index.asp**.

Here are a few other cleaning products that may help, though these include manual labor:

- **Zwipes Microfiber Cleaning Cloths™** — Highly absorbent and safe for all surfaces, including car exteriors, these cloths are durable, machine washable, and great for cleaning anything and everything. Available in packs of 36 for around $20, they can be split among your kitchen, bathrooms, garage, and basement and reused for all cleaning projects. The microfiber picks up everything, leaves no lint behind, and many claim that when combined with water, it works better than any other cleaner, even on glass. For additional information, see **www.zwipes.com/**.

- **Micro Mitt** — Attracting dust like a magnet, your entire house can be dusted with no cleaners using this mitt. It is machine washable and available in various sizes for a price of about $10 each. For more information, see **http:// magicmicrocloth.com/Magic-Micro-Mitt.htm**.

- **Palmolive Dish Wipes®** — These wipes come with a soft side and a scrubby side to quickly clean your dishes. Available in lemon or original scent, just get one wet, use it as needed, and dispose of it when finished. These add a little fun to dish duty, and your kids will enjoy using them as well.

There are a few other well-kept secrets that can assist you with your housekeeping tasks.

Consider these shortcuts whenever possible.

- **Hire a professional organizer** — If you are unsure of where to begin, hire a professional to come work along-side you in your home. This will jump start your project, and they can quickly provide solutions you may not eas-ily see for yourself. They offer various levels of assistance, from bringing in a team to do the work for you to serving as more of a consultant and outlining a plan for you to follow on your own. They also offer follow-up services to help your family change their overall behavior. The fee for a professional organizer is sometimes figured hourly, by the day, or per project. An average hourly rate ranges from $55 – $85 per hour.

- **Multitask** — Take advantage of any available minutes. If you are on the phone, grab a window cleaner wipe, and clean your patio windows. Wipe down a counter, or fold your clean laundry. Rearrange items on your bulletin board, or go through your stack of mail.

- **Add your seasonal or monthly tasks to your family cal-endar** — Tasks, such as changing the air filter, smoke alarm batteries, or cleaning the garbage disposal, can be forgot-ten if they are not placed on your family's radar. Let your computer remember these for you so you do not have to. Do the same for outdoor tasks, such as fertilizing the lawn, planting flowers, or adding chemicals to the swimming pool or hot tub.

The next section will look at ways to reduce trips to the store and ways to ensure you only buy what you need.

How to Reduce Shopping Trips and Costs

In America, it is estimated a family of four throws out almost $600 of groceries each year. This is due to poor planning, preparing too much food at a time, or improperly storing leftovers. You can learn to better manage the food that is prepared and discarded in your own home, becoming less wasteful in the process. Follow these tips to save money, time, and effort where your meals are concerned.

1. Make a grocery list, and stick to it. Check any recipes in advance for odd ingredients, and take a quick inventory of your cupboard and refrigerator so you do not buy duplicates. Get the kids to help with your list, and make them choose healthy snacks.

2. Buy only the amounts you will use, especially when buying produce and perishables. These items have a shorter shelf life so plan accordingly.

3. Serve small portions to your children, and let them come back for more if they choose to so that food is not wasted.

4. Have a plan for leftovers. Share with a neighbor or use to prepare other meals. Chop up bacon for salads, or make hash browns out of leftover baked potatoes, extending the benefits of the food that you purchase.

5. When placing your newest batch of groceries in the cabinet or refrigerator, rotate older items to the front to make sure they are used first.

6. Keep cookies, crackers, cereal, and chips in plastic bags to preserve their freshness. These items grow stale quickly when not closed properly.

7. Buy non-perishable items in bulk if you have the room to store them.

8. Many stores now offer a grocery delivery service. For a small fee, this can actually save you money because it prevents you from spontaneously buying items and forces you to stick within your budget.

9. To save money, match coupons to sales at particular stores, and shop on double or triple coupon days, which is where the store doubles or triples the value of each coupon. The Grocery Game™ is a service that does this for you, for a small membership fee, but those who use it say they instantly save several hundred dollars a month because the research is done for them. For more information on this service, visit **www.thegrocerygame.com**.

10. Pay for your groceries in cash. This keeps you under budget and prevents you from purchasing unneeded items.

Become a gift guru

If you have a large family, your children will constantly face the pressure of birthday parties and the need to purchase last-minute gifts. A good way to save money and to reduce shopping trips is to prepare for these events in advance by buying good gift items in bulk while on clearance. Though you already know the cautions associated with buying unnecessary items just because they are on sale, this method can work well for larger families with frequent gift-giving events to attend. Store these items in your gift wrap closet so you can quickly choose a gift, a card, the gift wrap, and be on your way to the party without an unnecessary trip to the store.

As you unclutter your home, place any items you come across that are unopened and can be re-gifted in this closet. Store items such as:

- Picture frames
- Candles and candle holders
- Holiday containers, such as salt and pepper shakers or lotion dispensers
- Decorative plaques or wall hangings
- Cookie jars
- Books/DVDs
- Stationery sets
- Unused gift cards — Make sure you have the date and amount marked on a sticky note attached to the gift card. Many expire after time or are charged a monthly fee, which essentially erases the value. If you are not sure of an amount or if it is valid, take it into the store, and they can swipe it and provide a receipt showing the current value of the card.

Then, consider purchasing other items along the way that could work well for a young girl or boy.

- Jump ropes
- Bubbles
- Kids' flashlights
- Rubber balls
- Sidewalk chalk
- Crayons and coloring books
- Decks of cards

- Slinkys or other small toys
- Stuffed animals

Purchase a box of generic greeting and birthday cards, and you will be set for any gifting occasion. You may also wish to hang a wall calendar on the door so you can mark important occasions, such as birthdays or anniversaries.

Giving gifts that matter to family and friends

Taking another approach to gift giving, specifically for your family and close friends, rather than rushing to buy the latest kitchen electronic or item seen on television, use these occasions to give gifts worth treasuring forever. You will find the process of pulling such a project together brings as much pleasure to the gift-giver as it does to the one who receives it.

The best anti-clutter news for all homes took place when pictures transferred from film to digital formats, simplifying the photo sharing and storing process. No longer do you end up with boxes of photos or negatives stored in your closets where no one can ever see them. With the ability to instantly view the photos, you can quickly delete bad photographs, removing the dreaded fingertip photos from your collection. You only print what you need, and photos can be quickly shared online where loved ones from all corners of the world can view them immediately. Edit your photos with free online programs to erase red eyes and shadows so every photo becomes a great one. You can also create unique personalized gifts with your digital photos.

Consider these gift ideas:

- Scrapbooks can be either digital or hand created. They help tell a complete story and work great as graduation gifts, sharing the first year of a baby's life, or showcasing a wedding story from the first date to the exchanging of the vows.

- Create a hardback book made up only of your photos and captions. They can be as small as 16 pages or as large as a coffee table book. For those who enjoy photography, creating a book of this magnitude can display years of work in a way that truly honors their talent.

- Make a photo collage poster. Rather than buying a poster at a particular event, take your own photos while attending that event, and create your own poster. Plan your photos in advance, taking pictures of the scoreboard at the end of a championship game; of your favorite team holding the trophy; of your family in the stands all decked out in team colors; and a close-up shot of the souvenir tickets.

- Design a personalized photo quilt or throw to remember a particular family reunion or special occasion.

- Some companies even offer a cartoon version of your photos. Create a comic book version of your family characters, and you will be bombarded with requests for additional copies. Some companies offer discounts for duplicate purchases so this could be a great gift for everyone in the family.

Other priceless gifts that take up little space but are well loved are listed below:

- If someone in your family is great with a video camera and knows how to edit film, you can create a great family video that includes interviews, birthday parties, past holiday celebrations, and other family milestones. Though a project of this magnitude is time consuming, a gift such as this will be treasured and can hold a large amount of memories in a small space.

- Transfer old home movies to DVD format. This allows you to separate the events in your lifetime into various "chapters," or scenes, so they can be found easily and watched regularly. You can make a DVD for each person in the family that showcases video footage of his or her own special moments. If you do not have time to devote to this project, you can use a company that offers this service, such as iMemories®, found at **www.imemories.com**.

CASE STUDY: SANDY JENNEY, ORGANIZE WITH SANDY

Sandy Jenney
Organize with Sandy
Johnstown, Ohio
OrganizewithSandy@yahoo.com
www.organizewithsandy.com
(740) 817-2203

Sandy Jenney grew up with the benefit of having both parents who were quite organized, passing down such skills to her long before Jenney recognized how they could help others. Somewhat new to the world of professional organizing, Jenney still serves as a pediatric nurse, an occupation she has loved for 28 years. This experience, along with the fact that she has raised eight children of her own, adds an extra level of awareness of the needs of children to the recommendations she makes for her clients. Her business, Organize with Sandy, opened in 2007, and she knows from experience that keeping a home organized and uncluttered becomes even more important when faced with medical challenges or for children with special needs.

Jenney loves to work with her clients in their own homes so she can teach them how to conquer their problems on their own. She sets up workable yet simple systems that empower her clients to continue the process once she is gone. She offers to take donation items to the local Salvation Army store for her clients so those items are out of the house by the end of the day. If left in the home, people are more likely to reconsider their decision and go back through the donation bags. Jenney also discourages garage sales, unless they are scheduled within a week or two, because many of her clients will hang onto items for a garage sale that never happens.

For those who say they do not have time to get organized, Jenney said, "It actually takes more time to be disorganized. Once you have removed the clutter out of your space, your mind will be less cluttered as well, giving a sense of peace."

Jenney designed her own job board for her family using a magnetic dry erase board and magnets made for attaching business cards. She cuts index cards to fit and writes her kids' names, attaching them to the sticky side of the magnet. Placing them in a row atop the magnetic board, this creates a column for each child. Then, she creates a magnet for each chore or task that needs to be done, assigning them to the column per child. The tasks can be as simple as "brush teeth" or as complex as "clean kitchen," but with the board in place, Jenney no longer had to be the one reminding her kids of their tasks. See photo below.

Jenney's favorite tip to offer her clients is this: "When uncluttering a room, bring in both black trash bags, as well as white ones. Use the black ones for trash, and the white ones for donations. This easily keeps them separated and will ensure you do not accidentally make 'trash' out of your donation bags."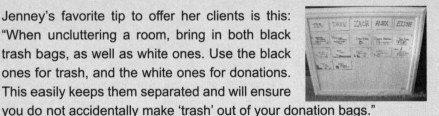

Next, this book will look at ways to properly honor your possessions that, to you, are priceless treasures. With the right approach, you can create room for these items in your home without allowing them to take over your space.

Chapter 15

Honoring Your Past without Destroying Your Future

· ·

One of the main reasons for keeping items even when there is no room to store them is because of the sentimental journey they take you on. As loved ones pass on, the presence of their belongings keep their memory alive. The sentimental value of their books, clothing, furniture, dishes, and other collectibles increase with time, and the thought of getting rid of their belongings brings a deep feeling of guilt. However, if you have no place for your grandmother's bequeathed piano, and no one in your family plays the piano, you are not letting your grandmother down by getting rid of it. Instead, display a photo of her playing the piano rather than rearranging your home around this large piece of furniture.

To recapture your home for your family to use, you must find a balance between sentimental and practical value. Pieces that hold sentimental value can add a great feel to your home, as long as you keep them in balance. Recognize that you are not honoring the memories of your loved ones by storing their treasures away in a box where they are never seen and that you do not love them any less by choosing to get rid of those items.

How to Handle Collectibles

Sentimental value is also a huge factor for the collector in your family. To the collector, the experience of obtaining those items one at a time is personal and unique. As the collection grows, it follows the owner through various stages in life. Like a valued toy or pet, it provides consistency and dependability. And, with many collectible items, the collection itself increases in value as it ages. However, a collection is most appreciated when it is displayed properly and not stowed away in a forgotten box in the attic or basement.

But, what should you do if you have a collector in the family? The majority of collectors do not have the luxury of a complete room devoted only to displaying their prized possessions so the goal is to find a way for the collection to peacefully coexist with your family. Make sure you control the collection and that it is not controlling you or your home. For collections of smaller items, you might wish to purchase a display case specifically for those items. Consider these possibilities as a way to display collections of value:

- Use a Plexiglas case, frames specifically designed for collections, or protective sheets in a notebook to display comic books or baseball cards.

- Display doll collections on shelves with doll furniture separating them. Label them if possible.

- Collector books work well for stamps, coins, and patches.

- Art Vinyl®, available at **www.artvinyl.com**, offers a frame made specifically for storing albums. The records slide out easily when it is time to play the record. This is a great way to decorate a listening room or den for the album collector.

- Display hats on a hat rack, stand, shelf, or by hanging them around the top edges of a wall.

- For cookie jars or teapots, hang a shelf 1 foot from the ceiling, and place them safely up there. You might also consider plant ledges or the top of your kitchen cabinets.

- Use window seats to display smaller collections of non-breakable items, such as stuffed animals, hand puppets, or rag dolls.

- Use an entertainment center to show movie or vintage television memorabilia. Display books with your beloved characters on the cover, framed photos, DVD cases, and magazine covers.

Tip #15

O
p
p
r
e
s
s

t
h
e

M
e
s
s

Create a Photo Gallery Wall

If you have a large empty wall available, consider creating a photo gallery wall. It is a great way for teens to showcase their memories throughout the year, displaying everything from photos, notes, movie tickets, greeting cards, and prom programs. By not using frames, you can keep it simple so you can add to the gallery throughout the year without having to adjust those items already in place.

- Measure your wall and divide it into equal parts.
- Cut six to eight 2-inch wide ribbons in equal lengths. Hang them 1 foot apart on your wall.
- Use double-sided foam tape to attach photos to your ribbons, trying to match sizes as much as possible. Some can be horizontal and some vertical.
- Decorate in between photo ribbons with movie tickets, advertisements, and other memorabilia.
- You might even print a date range to be taped on each ribbon or on the wall in between to show when those events took place.

Displaying military memorabilia

Those who have served in the military deserve a proper display of their accomplishments. Most soldiers do not readily share their own stories so it may be up to you, as a family member, to do it for them. Try the following suggestions:

- Use a shadowbox to display pins, badges, ribbon bars, dog tags, medals, and an insignia from their specific branch of service. Add newspaper headlines with any specific dates, and possibly their beret or ascot.

- Frame their military photo alongside any postmarked envelopes sent during time of service.

- Have the slogan or seal hand-painted on your display wall.

- Place an American flag in a flag case.

- Print any updates sent via e-mail during their time of service or the Internet in a book in chronological order, capturing their own stories in their own words.

Creative ways to display your keepsakes

Rather than storing the remnants of your most treasured memories in a sealed tub in the attic, try these suggestions for sharing those memories without overclutting your home with too many souvenirs.

1. Use shadowboxes to display groups of 3-D items. They come with a felt backing so you can attach items using adhesive fabric strips. These can hold photos, thin books, wedding ceremony programs, pressed flowers, printed napkins, greeting cards, clothing or uniforms, award certificates, and even jewelry or watches. They provide a wonderful way to tell a complete story of important events, such as weddings, vacations, or a season of baseball or other sports.

2. Purchase a four-panel room divider screen with photo holders on each side, and fill with meaningful photos. These help to separate rooms without walls, or you can even make one out of folding closet doors. After attaching them together, cover with corkboard or fabric, and attach your photos directly to the room divider. For a more decorative look, crisscross ribbons across each frame, and tuck photos behind the ribbons.

3. Decoupage copies of family photos onto a wooden serving tray. This can also work for wooden trunks. For di-

rections on how to do this, visit **http://the-artful-crafter. blogspot.com/2008/11/how-to-decoupage-family-pho- tos-onto.html**.

4. Install a photo ledge around the room that holds your framed pictures, and lean them against the wall. This keeps you from nailing numerous holes in the wall, and your pictures will always be straight.

5. Create a specific vacation display by storing sand and shells from your favorite beaches using tiny spice jars. La- bel each one and place in front of a large family photo with the date of your trip.

6. Make your own vacation poster by hanging a wall map, and tape vacation photos to the various places your family has been. Include the dates, and attach postcards around the edges of your display. Once it is complete, you can laminate it. Or, use the map as a background to a framed photo collage, and cut out photos, and add comment bub- bles to make it even more personal and humorous.

It is fun to personalize your home and fill it with things that mean something to you and your family. With a dose of creativity mixed with functionality, you can accomplish this without filling your home with clutter.

The next section will examine the best way to sort through, or- ganize, and distribute the mementos and treasures passed on to you from your loved ones.

CASE STUDY:
KELLI WILSON,
A SIMPLE PLAN CONSULTING

Kelli Wilson
Author, speaker,
clutter breakthrough expert
A Simple Plan Consulting
8445 Palmaire Way
Orangevale, CA 95662
kelli@asimpleplanconsulting.com
www.asimpleplanconsulting.com
916-765-6104

Kelli Wilson has been in the professional organization business for five years, but it was not until she attended a four-day conference for entrepre-  neurial women in August 2009 that she crossed the threshold into becoming an author. Her book, *The Clutter Break-through: Your Five-Step Solution to Freedom from Clutter Forever*, was released in the summer of 2010.

Wilson's approach to the problem of clutter is unique because she addresses it on a spiritual level. She studied the patterns of addictions for the past ten years, including the challenges for those with chronic disorganization problems, such as ADHD, brain injuries, and dementia. Wilson makes a difference in the lives of her clients who are strongly bothered by the thought of letting go of their things by helping them to understand the root of the problem.

"I am not a put-stuff-in-a-pretty-box type of organizer, at least not until my clients understand why they have all the stuff that they do," Wilson said.

Wilson finds that she does not need to recommend particular products for storage and organizational purposes. She finds when she enters her clients' homes that they have an abundance of organizational tools, such as bins and baskets, that have gone unused.

The largest obstacle to making a long-term improvement in the condition of the home that Wilson sees is one parent trying to do it all. When this is the case, failure, frustration, and exhaustion are sure to follow. She teaches her clients to get the entire family involved by working on projects together.

Wilson will continue to educate her clients on the many ways that clutter is the symptom of a much deeper need. If they do not free themselves from the mental and emotional clutter, they will soon find themselves trapped by their physical clutter once again. She knows it is a painful process, but walking with her clients through the process is what she finds so rewarding.

Inheriting Family Treasures

With aging parents or other relatives, it is important to establish a plan of action for their belongings long before it is time to act on that plan. For example, if you are moving parents into a special care facility, your focus should be on them and on ways to ease them into their new environment rather than on what to do with their stuff. Find out in advance what they wish to be done with their prized possessions so you will not be left wondering. Many families are left to sort through a houseful of stuff after the loss of a loved one when they are not emotionally ready to handle the decisions that must be made.

Use family gatherings to begin sorting through items and taking inventory so you at least become aware of what is there and what can be discarded in advance. If you begin the process of gradually de-cluttering early on, moving a parent will become much easier to manage. Most older family members have not been in their attic or basement in years to even recall what is stored there. As you go through the items, watch for things that may be of value and offer personal relevance regarding your family's history. Separate items into papers and books, photos, clothing, furniture, and other objects. Assign a different person to go through each category so the job does not become too overwhelming.

If you have a great amount of antique furniture, paintings, books, and even historical documents, bring in an appraiser to determine the true value of items so you can make the best decisions. Protect photos and historical documents by storing them in acid-free containers in a place that is neither too humid (basement) or too dry and hot (attic).

If it quickly becomes clear that you must donate items, choose a charity that means something to your loved one. Consider donations to local museums, but make sure you are always aware of exactly what you are donating and what the true value of it is. Never donate a valuable item by accident.

The process of distributing the belongings of an elderly relative is painful regardless of whether it is done before or after a death. It is difficult to let go of those memories, but the memories live in the hearts of the ones who loved that person, never in the things they leave behind. It is your choice whether to keep any inherited items, but try to think of what may be valuable 30 years down the road. If you were writing the history of your family, what would you need to keep in order to properly share your story? You must find the balance between creating a museum in your home and carelessly getting rid of things of value.

It would be much easier to de-clutter the home if there were no emotional attachments to your things, but life would also seem quite empty without your sentimental journeys. By cherishing the memories and displaying them in the right way, your home can be a perfect blend of who you are, what your family needs in order to function in this day and time, and just a touch of history that makes your family unique.

Conclusion

Unclutter Your Mind

K eeping your home, your life, and your family clutter-free requires both discipline and diligence. However, once you realize how quickly a cluttered home zaps your energy and causes even more fatigue, you will be willing to put forth the effort to stay on top of it. Taking junk mail straight to the trash or recycle bin requires as much work as laying it on a table to deal with later. Placing dishes in the dishwasher requires the same effort as taking them to the sink and leaving them for later.

Your mind gets clogged with silent to-do lists and keeps you from enjoying the moment at hand. Somewhat comparable to renovating a house, it is difficult to enjoy the changes that are already made if you are focused only on what remains to be done.

De-cluttering Your Life

This book started with taking inventory in your own home environment to determine what hinders your desire for an uncluttered home. With families, it is a challenge to keep everyone on the same page, but it is worth the effort. By this point, you have a better idea of the strengths and weaknesses within your own family. With time and effort, you can gradually remove each hurdle, and the process will no longer feel like an obstacle course. Simplify whenever and wherever possible.

You now know the truth about clutter: It steals your joy. It is a magnet for additional clutter. It zaps your energy. It represents your own procrastination, revealing the assorted stacks of leftovers you simply were not ready to deal with. It fills your mind with negative thoughts of failure the moment you walk through the door. A cluttered lifestyle has the same effect, and this type of unneeded clutter takes on many forms. Clutter equals all the things you are not yet ready to deal with, and it can stack up just like your unwanted junk mail.

As with any cleaning project, be prepared to make a bit of a mess before you notice any improvement. If you were cleaning out your closet, you would pull everything out and start from the beginning. Determine what still fits, what has not been worn in years, and what is damaged beyond repair. The process of de-cluttering is rewarding because it strengthens your self-discipline and restores a sense of control where you once felt overwhelmed. As with any of your possessions, make sure you own them rather than them owning you.

Once you remove the clutter from all areas of your life, it frees you to pay attention to the things that matter most. Entering a neat and tidy space at the end of the day does not zap your energy but refreshes you and frees you to become more creative, to take the time to read a book, or to discover a new craft or hobby. The creative process, whether it is preparing a meal, writing a letter to a friend, or rearranging a room, brings satisfaction and spurs more creative energy.

Beneath the clutter in your home, you may discover several hidden talents among your family members. The greatest reward for sticking to this plan is to unbury those talents, freeing your family to become more creative and enjoy their surroundings rather than feeling trapped by them.

Finding the Right Balance

The thrill of getting your home under control pales in comparison to that of maintaining it from that point forward. Imagine going through each day without stressing over the condition of your home. A well-managed home combined with well-trained occupants will almost make it seem as if it is cleaning itself. As the experts featured in our case studies expressed, with the right organizational system and by removing the excess stuff, maintaining your new environment is easy.

Focus on the family, not the mess

As a parent, your greatest struggle may be to let go of control of the situation. If your kids make the effort to clean but their standards do not match your own, reward the effort and raise the standards a little at a time. In any situation, no one likes to be inspected on a regular basis and be told their work is not good enough.

Any time spent in your home should be valued for all members. Make sure you are not bombarding your family with a to-do list as soon as they walk in the door. Ask them how their day was, and listen to the answers to the end. It is so easy for a parent to become preoccupied with the next thing that must be done on the schedule that they forget to focus on the family itself. Never make a child feel that the house, carpet, wood floors, or the contents of the home are more important than your child. The only reason to have a nice home is to provide your family with the best environment possible as they grow up. Although this easily requires them to learn to care for their own belongings and pitch in to help on a regular basis, you want them to always feel at home in their home.

Your true reward in improving the home environment is that it frees you to spend quality time with your family and friends. No longer will you fear the moment a friend drops by unannounced. No longer will you be too preoccupied with chores to pay attention to your family as they come in the door. By making them a part of the process, you may find that your best conversations take place while working together on a project like folding laundry, unloading the dishwasher, making the bed, or baking cookies.

Trust your new system to work for you, and invest your time and energy into being the spouse, parent, sibling, son or daughter, aunt or uncle, or friend you always desired to be. Quality time spent with those you love the most is much more important and long lasting than having a spotless home. Learning to do both well creates the perfect balance and leads to a greatly satisfying lifestyle.

Bibliography

1-800-Got Junk (**www.1800gotjunk.com**) Accessed June 21, 2010.

A&E Television Network *Hoarders* (**www.aetv.com/hoarders**) Accessed on Feb. 7, 2010.

Aguirre, Sarah. About.com: Housekeeping "10 Laundry Disasters and How to Help Clothes Recover" (**http://housekeeping.about.com/od/laundry/a/laundrydisaster.htm**) Accessed May 10, 2010.

Allied Van Lines, Inc. "Garage Sale Tips" (**www.allied.com/moving-tips/garage-sales.aspx**) Accessed on May June 3, 2010.

Art Vinyl, Ltd. "Play and Display" (**www.artvinyl.com**) Accessed on March 9, 2010.

BabyCenter, LLC. "Childproofing Your Kitchen" (**www.babycenter.com/0_childproofing-your-kitchen_755.bc**) Accessed on May 14, 2010.

"Bathroom Cleaning Tips," Lifetips.com (**http://cleaning.lifetips.com/cat/7435/bathroom-cleaning/index.html**) Accessed on April 14, 2010.

Becker, Joshua. "The Statistics of Clutter," Becoming Minimalist (**www.becomingminimalist.com/2010/01/19/the-statistics-of-clutter**) Accessed on March 3, 2010.

Bell, Stephanie. "Tips for Speed Cleaning Your House," Associated Content (**www.associatedcontent.com/article/2473516/tips_for_speed_cleaning_your_house.html?cat=30**) Accessed on June 3, 2010.

Bergen, Eileen. "How to Decoupage Family Photos onto Wooden Trays," The Artful Crafter (**http://the-artful-crafter.blogspot.com/2008/11/how-to-decoupage-family-photos-onto.html**) Accessed on May 11, 2010.

Berkus, Nate. "Furniture for Small Spaces," Oprah.com. (**www.oprah.com/home/Furniture-for-Small-Spaces**) Accessed on Feb. 3, 2010.

Books for Soldiers (**http://booksforsoldiers.com/**) Accessed on May 21, 2010.

Buffalo Exchange (**www.buffaloexchange.com**) Accessed on May 28, 2010.

Career Gear (**http://careergear.org/**) Accessed on May 21, 2010.

Caruso, Inya Bort. "Good Ideas for Basement Storage," Everything.com (**www.everything.com/good-ideas-basement-storage/#axzz0lC2lgetl**) Accessed on June 10, 2010.

"Causes of Hoarding," The International OCD Foundation (**www.ocfoundation.org/hoarding/causes.aspx**) Accessed on March 10, 2010.

Children's Orchard (**www.childrensorchard.com**) Accessed on May 28, 2010.

"Clean Up Your Kid's Clutter" Right @ Home. (**www.rightathome.com/Cleaning/Articles/Pages/ CleanUpYourKidsClutter.aspx**) Accessed on March 28, 2010.

Closet and Storage Concepts (**www.closetandstorageconcepts. com/closet.htm**) Accessed on July 30, 2010.

Closet Organizers Kits.com (**http://closetorganizerskits.com/ hanging-jewelry-organizer-black-37-pockets-organize.asp**) and (**http://closetorganizerskits.com/kids-daily-activity-organizer- 6-shelf-hanging-closet.asp**) Accessed on April 17, 2010.

ClosetOrganizerSource.com. "Laundry Organizers" (**www. closetorganizersource.com/laundry-organizers/1914+1922.cfm**) Accessed on March 22, 2010.

College Hunks Hauling Junk (**www.1800junkusa.com**) Accessed on July 28, 2010.

Comfort House (**www.comforthouse.com/dustpan. html?feed=ysw**) and (**www.comforthouse.com/dirtdevil4. html**) Accessed on July 28, 2010.

The Container Store, Inc. (**www.containerstore.com/shop/ closet/accessoryStorage/handbags?productId=10005482**) and (**www.containerstore.com/shop/kitchen/cabinetOrganizers/up perCabinets?productId=10023942**) Accessed on May 18, 2010.

Cozi (**www.cozi.com**) Accessed on June 19, 2010.

Craigslist. "Avoiding Scams and Fraud" (**www.craigslist.org/ about/safety**) Accessed on July 7, 2010.

The Daily Green. "10 Easy Ways to Reduce Food Waste" (**www. thedailygreen.com/going-green/community-tips/reduce-food- waste-460708#ixzz0sRBjszEt**) Accessed on June 23, 2010.

DirectMail.com (**www.directmail.com/directory/mail_ preference/**) Accessed on July 1, 2010.

"Donate Used Items to Support the Needy," Squidoo (**www. squidoo.com/donate-used-items-to-support-the-needy**) Accessed on May 24, 2010.

Dormco.com (**www.dormco.com/Fold_Away_Futon_Dorm_ Furniture_Seating_p/dormco-3101nb.htm**) Accessed on March 31, 2010.

Dornob. "Interactive Interiors: Convertible Kids' Bedroom Furniture" (**http://dornob.com/interactive-interiors-convertible-kids-bedroom-furniture/**) Accessed on March 31, 2010.

Dress for Success Worldwide (**www.dressforsuccess.org**) Accessed on June 23, 2010.

The Droodle (**www.thedroodle.com**) Accessed on May 17, 2010.

Earth911.com. "Recycling 101 – The Recyclopedia" (**http://earth911.com/recycling**) Accessed on July 2, 2010.

EasyClosets.com, LLC. (**www.easyclosets.com**) Accessed on April 21, 2010.

eHow. "How to Display Family Mementos" (**www.ehow.com/ how_2124824_display-family-mementos.html**) Accessed on May 28, 2010.

eHow. "How to Do Laundry" (**www.ehow.com/how_46_ laundry.html**) Accessed on May 5, 2010.

eHow. "How to Donate Your Car" (**www.ehow.com/ how_107456_donate-car.html**) Accessed on May 23, 2010.

Elledge, James. "Clean Desk Policy" Today's Facility Manager. (**www.todaysfacilitymanager.com/fm_expert159.php**) Accessed on May 28, 2010.

The Family Handyman. "How to Keep Pests Out of Your House" (**www.familyhandyman.com/DIY-Projects/Outdoor-Projects/Yard/Pests/how-to-keep-pests-out-of-your-house/Step-By-Step**) Accessed on June 11, 2010.

Fields, Laura Leigh. "Reflections: Losing a Storage Unit," Helium (**www.helium.com/items/852236-reflections-losing-a-storage-unit**) Accessed on Feb. 11, 2010.

"Get a Better Night's Sleep Without Electronic Media," Life Hacker (**http://lifehacker.com/293625/get-a-better-nights-sleep-without-electronic-media**) Accessed on August 31, 2010.

Giveyourstuffaway.com. "Give Your Stuff Away – Formerly known as Curb Day" (**http://giveyourstuffaway.com**) Accessed on June 10, 2010.

Good Housekeeping. "Kids' Room: Easy Organizing and Decorating Tips" (**www.goodhousekeeping.com/home/organizing/kids-room-organize-decor**) Accessed on April 22, 2010.

TheGroceryGame.com (**www.thegrocerygame.com**) Accessed on June 11, 2010.

Giullian, Marianne. "Do You Know the Real Cost of Storage Units?" TheDollarStretcher.com (**www.stretcher.com/stories/07/07apr16b.cfm**) Accessed on Feb. 21, 2010.

Habitat for Humanity International. "Restore Resale Outlets" (**www.habitat.org/env/restores.aspx**) Accessed on June 14, 2010.

Huge Drive (**www.hugedrive.com**) Accessed on June 3, 2010.

iMemories (**www.iMemories.com**) Accessed on May 11, 2010.

iResQ Purchase Program (**www.iresq.com/skin/frontend/ default/iresq/purchaseform.phtml**) Accessed on May 15, 2010.

iRobot Corporation Cleaning Robots (**http://store.irobot.com/ home/index.jsp**) Accessed on June 14, 2010.

iSoldit on eBay (**http://877isoldit.com/**) Accessed on June 11, 2010.

JCPenney Company, Inc. "Allie Day Bed" (**www2.jcpenney. com/jcp/X6.aspx?GrpTyp=PRD&ItemID=15a2132&Ntt=allie+ day+bed&hdnOnGo=true&Ne=4+6+1031+8+18+904+949+833 &submit%20search.y=0&SearchString=allie+day+bed&subm it%20search.x=0&N=4294959029&Nao=0&SO=0&PSO=0&Cm CatId=searchresults**) Accessed on Feb. 12, 2010.

JustJunk.com (**www.justjunk.com**) Accessed on June 12, 2010.

Kidflicks.org (**www.kidflicks.org/?page_id=3**) Accessed on May 14, 2010.

Kitchensource.com (**www.kitchensource.com/cau/na- appliancegarage.htm**) Accessed on April 28, 2010.

Kober, Jeff. "At Disney, Everyone Picks up Trash!" Mouse Planet (**www.mouseplanet.com/6971/At_Disney_Everyone_Picks_ Up_Trash**) Accessed on Feb. 10, 2010.

Magic Micro Mitt (**http://magicmicrocloth.com/Magic-Micro-Mitt.htm**) Accessed on May 28, 2010.

Maister, Kathy. "How to Load a Dishwasher," Kathy Maister's Startcooking.com. (**http://startcooking.com/blog/37/How-to-Load-a-Dishwasher**) Accessed on April 11, 2010.

Murray, Stacey Agin. "6 Tips for Organizing Your Refrigerator," Organized Artistry, LLC (**www.organizedartistry.com/orgofridge.html**) Accessed on April 30, 2010.

Nabou.com. "Clothing Storage Tips" (**www.garmentcare.info/maintaining_your_wardrobe_storage/clothing_storage_tips.html**) Accessed on May 13, 2010.

New Eyes for the Needy (**http://neweyesfortheneedy.com/impact/shipping.html**) Accessed on May 15, 2010.

Norton Online Family (**https://onlinefamily.norton.com/familysafety/loginStart.fs**) Accessed on June 3, 2010.

Off the Wall Beds (**www.offthewallbeds.com/bedsspecial.html**) Accessed on Feb. 18, 2010.

Once Upon a Child (**www.onceuponachild.com/**) Accessed on May 11, 2010.

Organize-It. (**http://storage.organizeit.com/storage/roll-out%20shelves**) Accessed on May 11, 2010.

Pasis, Dena. "How to Organize your Kitchen Pantry," About.com (**http://personalorganizing.about.com/od/kitchenorganization/ht/KitchenPantry.htm**) Accessed April 14, 2010.

Perets, Abbi. "No More Clutter: Four Tips for Organizing the Kids' Bathroom," SheKnows. (**www.sheknows.com/articles/808611/four-tips-for-organizing-the-kids-bathroom**) Accessed on March 24, 2010.

Pickup 2 Sell, LLC. (**www.pickup2sell.com/**)
Accessed on May 31, 2010.

Plato's Closet (**www.platoscloset.com/how-it-works**)
Accessed on June 20, 2010.

Play it Again Sports (**www.playitagainsports.com**)
Accessed on June 20, 2010.

"Playing it Safe with Hazardous Waste," Nashville Government
Metro Public Works Division of Waste Management
(**www.nashville.gov/Recycle/pdfs/HHWBrochure.pdf**)
Accessed on June 10, 2010.

Poggy's Kids Custom Furniture (**www.poggyskids.com**)
Accessed on March 17, 2010.

"Poisoning as a Leading Cause of Injury Deaths,"
National Conference of State Legislatures (**www.ncsl.org/
IssuesResearch/Health/PoisonControlCenters/tabid/13863/
Default.aspx**) Accessed on May 28, 2010.

Prison Book Program (**www.prisonbookprogram.org/
otherprograms.php**) Accessed on June 21, 2010.

Reconnect (**http://reconnectpartnership.com/howitworks.php**)
Accessed on June 15, 2010.

Reidel, Dela. "Good Old Attic Storage Techniques," Calfinder
Nationwide Remodelers. (**www.calfinder.com/blog/tips/good-
old-attic-storage-techniques/**) Accessed on April 30, 2010.

Schorn, Daniel. "Andy's Personality Quiz – Are you
Type A or Type B?" CBS News (**www.cbsnews.com/
stories/2007/06/14/60minutes/rooney/main2930028.shtml**)
Accessed on February 3, 2010.

Scrubbing Bubbles Automated Shower Cleaner
(**www.automaticshowercleaner.com/index.asp**)
Accessed on June 19, 2010.

Seldin, Naomi. "Death by Hoarding," *Times Union* (**http://blog.
timesunion.com/simplerliving/death-by-hoarding/3637/**)
Accessed on March 3, 2010.

Self Storage Association (**www.selfstorage.org/SSA/Home/AM/
ContentManagerNet/ContentDisplay.aspx?Section=Home&C
ontentID=4228**) Accessed on Feb. 23, 2010.

Small Wonder (**http://smallwonder.info/**)
Accessed on June 11, 2010.

Snappy Auctions (**www.snappyauctions.com/index.php**)
Accessed on June 15, 2010.

SofiaMaria, "How to Recognize Signs of a Shopping Addiction,"
eHow (**www.ehow.com/how_4858218_recognize-signs-of-
shopping-addiction.html**) Accessed on March 29, 2010.

Space Bag (**www.spacebag.com/**) Accessed on April 4, 2010.

Sports Gift, Inc. (**www.sportsgift.org/donate_all-sports.html**)
Accessed on May 25, 2010.

Staples Soul Recycling Program (**www.staples.com/sbd/
content/about/soul/recycling.html**) Accessed on May 25, 2010.

Steinwachs, Marie. "Store Hazardous Products Safely,"
University of Missouri Extension (**http://extension.missouri.
edu/publications/DisplayPub.aspx?P=WM6005**)
Accessed on April 11, 2010.

Style Network *Clean House* blog (**www.mystyle.com/mystyle/ shows/cleanhouse/blog/index.jsp?categoryName=clean_ house&pageNum=2**) Accessed Aug. 31, 2010.

"Summary of the Resource Conservation and Recovery Act," U.S. Environmental Protection Agency (**www.epa.gov/lawsregs/ laws/rcra.html**) Accessed on June 11, 2010.

Taliercio, Nell. "10 Easy Steps to an Organized Home Office," Lifeorganizers.com (**http://lifeorganizers.com/Organize-Your-Home/The-Organized-Home-Office/Easy-HomeOffice-Organizing.html**) Accessed on June 3, 2010.

Trattner, Douglas. "Garage Storage Solutions," HGTV. (**www. hgtv.com/organizing/garage-organization-ideas/index.html**) Accessed on June 15, 2010.

Urbanska, Wanda. "Mind Over Mess: How clearing the clutter out of your space can help you clear your head, too," *Navigations.*,2007 (**www.simplelivingtv.net/files/May07_EL_ WandaArticle.pdf**) Accessed on May 20, 2010.

Whelan, Susan. "How to Clean a Bathroom and Keep it Tidy: Establishing a Maintenance and Cleaning Routine for Bathrooms," Suite101.com (**http://home-organization.suite101. com/article.cfm/bathroom_cleaning_plan**) Accessed on April 23, 2010.

Wong, Max. "5 Ways Self Storage Units are More Sad Museums than Savvy Solutions" Wisebread. (**www.wisebread.com/5-ways-self-storage-units-are-more-sad-museums-than-savvy-solutions**) Accessed on February 23, 2010.

Zwipes. (**www.zwipes.com**) Accessed on May 24, 2010.

Author Biography

Janet Morris Grimes writes from the perspective of a wife, parent, and employee who knows how difficult it is to balance it all and do any of it well. After downsizing from a 3,200-square-foot home to a 1,000-square-foot apartment four states away, she learned the hard way how to let go of stuff that owns you and that without a plan of action, clutter will find you. "Freedom," she says, "is a great place to live. The less you own, the less there is to take care of." Janet writes on a variety of topics, including faith, family, and the writing process.

Index

A

Appliances, 58, 191, 195, 224, 228, 241

Attic, 45, 50, 117, 132-133, 142, 150, 197, 199-201, 203-204, 206, 226, 260, 263, 266-267, 280

B

Basement, 45, 50, 68, 81, 86, 117, 132-133, 150, 197, 199-201, 205-206, 226, 233, 250, 260, 266-267, 274

Basket, 28, 72, 85, 87, 92, 96-97, 101-102, 109, 122, 129, 135, 143-144, 153, 159-161, 164-165, 168, 170, 172, 186, 195, 209-211, 247-248

Bathroom, 74, 90-91, 102, 107, 109, 113, 116, 118, 135, 146, 157-167, 169-173, 273, 279, 282

Bed, 35, 40, 50, 66, 85, 89-91, 97, 108, 116, 132, 136, 142-145, 147-148, 176, 272, 278

Bedroom, 29, 68, 85, 90, 95, 102, 116, 118, 120-121, 134, 136-138, 142-147, 151, 155, 157, 161, 197, 233, 276

Bin, 40, 45, 98, 135, 151, 186, 230, 237, 249, 269

Books, 26, 41, 45, 71, 82-85, 89-90, 96, 116, 129, 140-141, 144, 148-149, 155, 183, 193, 204, 209, 217, 222, 228, 230, 254, 259, 261, 263, 266 267, 271

C

Cabinets, 30, 79, 81, 85-86, 89, 96, 145, 158-161, 164, 166, 172, 181, 184-185, 187, 189, 191, 202, 208, 234, 242, 261

Car, 30, 35-36, 126, 148, 178, 196-197, 207, 209-210, 220, 237, 250, 276

Charity, 48, 70-71, 123, 191, 218, 220, 267

Checklist, 12, 20, 40, 79, 83-84, 146, 171, 178, 229

Closet, 19, 58, 82, 84, 87-88, 91-92, 95, 99, 102-103, 114-121, 123-132, 134-137, 146, 151, 155, 161, 165-166, 168, 172-173, 176, 216, 225, 253-254, 263, 270, 275, 280

Clothes, 17, 21, 28, 35, 38, 47, 70-71, 73, 85, 100-114, 116-117, 120-121, 123, 125-127, 129, 134, 145-147, 149, 168, 178, 229-230, 273

Collectibles, 259-260

Color code, 110

Commitment, 32, 64-65, 69, 146, 178, 222, 227, 229

Computer, 145, 211, 231, 236, 239-240, 246, 251

Consignment, 113, 123, 194, 224-225, 227

Cosmetics, 165, 171-173

D

Desk, 31-32, 34, 36-37, 85, 90, 93-94, 145, 147, 150-151, 173, 233-236, 238, 277

Dining room, 78

Dish, 105, 152, 176, 179, 186, 188, 250-251

Display, 63, 95, 114, 125, 127, 136, 144, 151, 154, 230-231, 256, 259-264, 273, 276

Donate, 44-45, 48, 55, 64, 71, 121, 123, 128, 130, 190-191, 194, 214, 217-218, 232, 235, 267, 276, 281

Door, 16, 19, 28, 61, 67, 73, 80-84, 86-88, 110, 112, 116, 126, 129-130, 134, 136, 139, 149, 157, 165, 167-168, 170, 173, 176, 180-181, 183, 186-188, 190-191, 194, 201, 204, 210, 216, 246, 255, 270, 272

E

eBay, 226-227, 278

Electronics, 45, 52, 161, 165, 178, 203, 214, 217, 226, 231

Entryway, 29, 84, 86-88

Equipment, 17, 29, 46, 49-50, 81, 86, 92, 119, 145, 150, 203, 206, 208, 217-218, 226, 228, 231

F

Family meeting, 65-68

Family room, 50, 68, 83-84, 91-92, 97, 109, 157, 167, 175, 196, 233

Floor, 21, 35, 40, 70-71, 74, 77, 79, 81, 83-87, 90, 100, 102-103, 116-117, 130, 133, 142-144, 162, 168, 170, 176, 180, 189-190, 202, 204, 206, 210, 228, 249

Food, 17, 66, 80, 98, 114, 133, 179-182, 189-192, 195, 197, 205, 212, 252, 275

Freezer, 180-183

Furniture, 26, 31-32, 40, 42, 45, 47, 49-50, 55-56, 58, 61, 79-80, 82, 84, 86, 88-91, 97, 114, 143-145, 147-148, 194, 204, 206, 225-226, 228, 230, 247, 259, 261, 266-267, 274, 276, 280

G

Games, 33, 37, 92, 94, 96, 119, 134, 137-138, 150, 224, 226, 228, 235, 239

Garage, 30, 41, 46, 50, 68, 81, 86, 123, 179, 191, 199, 201, 206-208, 212, 226-229, 249-250, 258, 273, 282

Gift, 64, 116, 137, 218, 253-257, 281

Goal, 20, 23, 28, 31-32, 45, 62, 64, 66, 69, 72-73, 97, 140-141, 169, 192, 260

H

Hamper, 71-72, 85, 100-103, 126, 146-147, 168, 170

Hoarding, 33, 41-42, 51-52, 194, 274, 281

Homework, 32-33, 91-94, 142, 146, 176, 194, 238-239

Hooks, 84-86, 88, 116-117, 128-129, 153-154, 162, 169-170, 234, 246

J

Jewelry, 90, 126-127, 153-155, 224, 263

K

Kitchen, 30, 50, 58, 72, 81, 84-85, 94, 160, 162, 173, 175-177, 181, 184, 186-193, 195-197, 228, 245, 247, 250, 255, 258, 261, 273, 275, 279

L

Laundry, 28, 40, 74, 78, 85, 98-106, 108-111, 114, 143, 153, 155, 159, 162, 170, 190, 209-210, 238, 247-248, 251, 272, 273, 275-276

Laundry room, 40, 78, 85, 100, 102, 109, 153, 159, 190, 238

Linens, 40, 50, 91, 99, 134, 136

Living room, 26, 48, 68, 83-84, 91

M

Mail, 28, 41, 82, 84, 86-88, 194, 236-238, 242-243, 251, 269-270, 276

Model home, 78-79

O

Odors, 32-33, 98, 105, 107, 133, 158, 178, 183, 203

Office, 31, 149, 193, 218, 232-236, 238, 241, 282

P

Packrat, 41-42

Pantry, 81, 114, 116, 189, 191, 195, 279

Personality, 13, 19, 31-32, 34-37, 77, 280

Pests, 133, 178, 200-203, 206, 277

Pets, 31, 33, 78, 80, 97-98, 133, 208, 229, 249

R

Recycle, 45, 213-214, 217, 221-222, 232, 237, 269, 280

Refrigerator, 82, 84, 91, 176-183, 187-188, 190, 252, 279

Repair, 48, 105-106, 122, 127, 130, 224, 270

Reward, 38, 66, 71-72, 123, 171, 271-272

S

Schedule, 17, 29, 40, 70, 94, 100, 109, 151, 161, 194, 229, 239-240, 245-246, 272

Seasonal, 116, 122-123, 126, 131-133, 212, 251

Self storage, 54, 281-282

Sell, 51, 55-56, 60, 79, 121, 123, 181-182, 194, 224, 226-229, 232, 280

Shelves, 26, 78-79, 81, 83, 85-86, 89, 91, 94, 96, 116-117, 123-125, 127-128, 130-131, 134-135, 137-138, 144-145, 149-150, 155, 160, 165-166, 180, 184-186, 189-190, 192, 202, 206, 234, 261

Shoes, 17-19, 29, 36, 48, 67, 72, 77-78, 84-85, 87-88, 107, 111, 116-117, 119-120, 122, 125-126, 129-130, 149, 194

Shopping, 12, 57-60, 178-179, 252-253, 281

Sock, 110-111, 133, 153, 165

Stains, 47, 80-81, 99, 101, 103, 107, 128, 162-163

Sticky note, 71, 119, 135, 254

Storage, 40, 46, 54-57, 80-81, 87-91, 94-95, 99, 114-119, 122-125, 129, 131-133, 145, 149-151, 164-165, 172, 176, 180, 184, 186-187, 189, 197, 199-200, 203-204, 208, 212, 234, 240, 265, 274-275, 277, 279-282

Stuffed animals, 96-97, 129, 150, 254-255, 261

Supplies, 70, 83, 85, 88, 93-95, 97, 137-138, 149-150, 158-161, 166, 172, 179, 187, 190, 202, 212

T

Towel, 35, 87, 105-106, 109, 136, 154, 165, 169-170, 187, 197, 211

Toys , 17, 28, 38, 50, 58, 71-72, 78, 80, 82-83, 86, 92, 94, 96-98, 120, 129, 135, 145, 147, 149-150, 171, 194, 224, 228, 230-231, 254-255